536.6015

Prue Francis

Plate 1: Normal Ring Neck Parrakeets
(Left: Female Right: Male)

Plate 2: Ring Neck Parrakeets; Lutino Male
Blue Female

CONTENTS

FOREWORD

RING-NECKED PARRAKEETS are one of the most widely kept birds. They are lively, aggressive creatures living in an aviary as they would in the wild – squabbling and flying around, and enjoying life in general.

With the many new Mutations interest continues to grow. Colours unheard of a few years ago are now available. We now wonder what will be next.

As an amateur bird-keeper I have tried to explain in fairly simple language, the history of Ring-Necks and how they are managed. The works of pioneers in breeding have been consulted and, where appropiate, have been quoted.

My grateful thanks are offered to those who supplied photographs or other material. Where appropiate the originators have been contacted, although in some cases this has not been possible. Prue Francis painted the originals for the colour plates based on birds owned by the author and other fanciers. The result is both artistic and informative.

In presenting facts based on personal experiences it is necessary to try to steer a course which suits the beginner and those with experience, this has its problems, but hopefully this approach will suit most readers. If any reader feels that there are facts which should be added then I would be pleased to receive suggestions.

Please try to remember that these magnificent birds give us many hours of enjoyment and interest. They deserve the best treatment we can give them in terms of food, accommodation and general environment.

January 1990   J. Batty

1

PARROTS AND PARROT-LIKE BIRDS

THE FAMILY GROUP*

Parrots belong to the order *Psittaciformes* and are grouped into the family known as Psittacidae. Within this family there are different groups of species (around 330) which are further broken into around 60 genera.
A further classification is the division into *sub-families* such as:

1. NESTORINAE – covers the Kaka and Kea parrots from New Zealand.

2. STRIGOPINAE – includes the Owl Parrot or Kakapo.

3. CYCLOPSITTACINAE genus PSITTACULIROSTRIS which contains five species originating from New Guinea, dwarf–like (around 4 to 7 inches, 10 to 18cm) and believed to be related to the Lories.

4. PLATYCERCINAE– which covers a wide range of species (29) which include the Rosellas.

5. CACATUINAE – covers the cockatoos of which there are some l6 species. It includes the popular Cockatiels.

6. MICROPSITTINAE– which includes six species of pygmy parrot, (around 4in (lOcm) which use their feathers to support themselves climbing trees.

7 LORIINAE which includes around 60 species of brush tongued parrots known as Lories and Lorikeets which feed on liquids (nectars) rather than seeds.

8. PSITTACINAE– consisting of the bulk of the parrots ranging from quite small birds such as Love Birds to the giants such as Amazon and

*Other Classifications are possible

Grey
Parrot

Blue-fronted
Amazon

Ring
-necked
Parrakeet

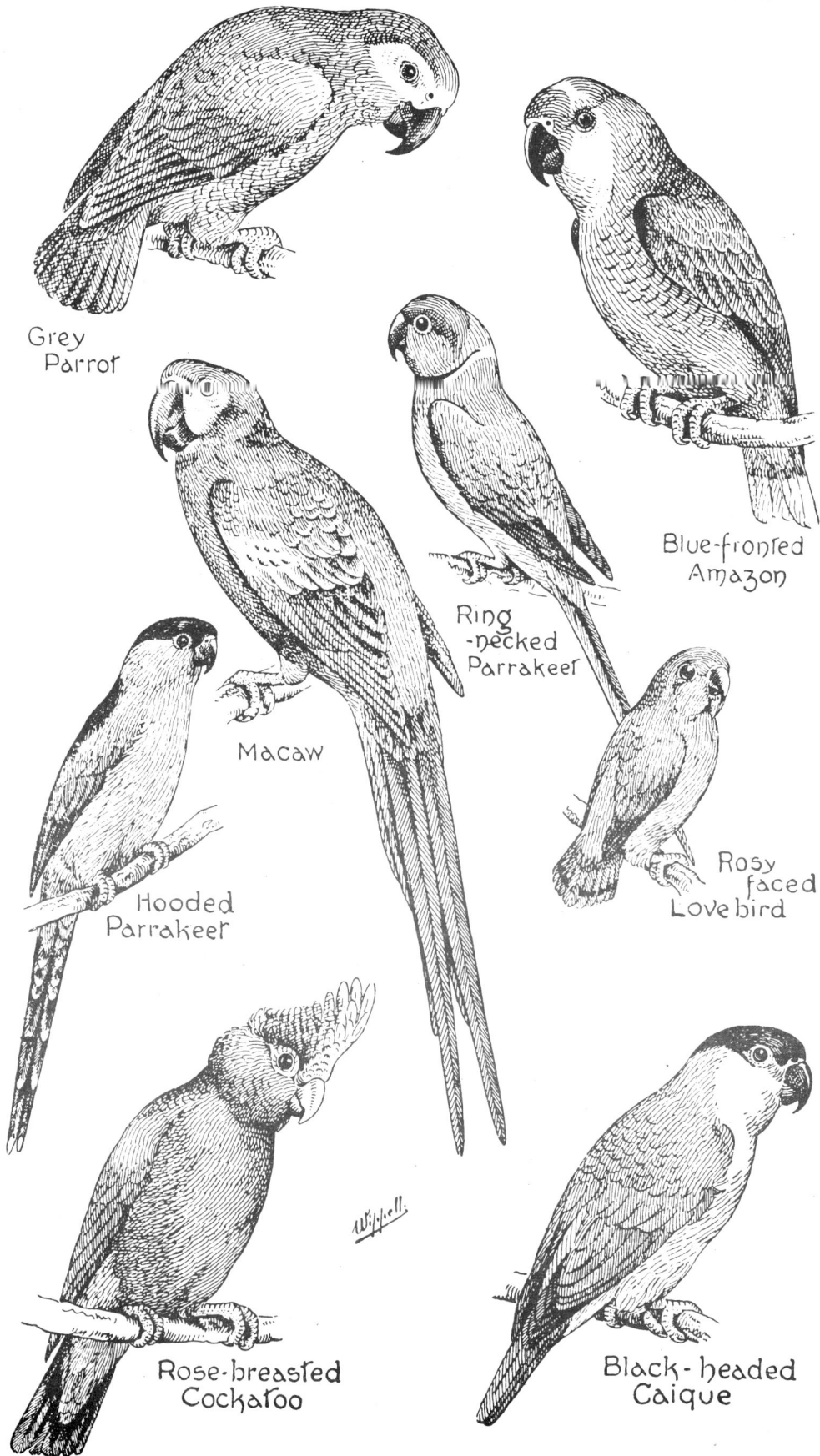

Macaw

Hooded
Parrakeet

Rosy
faced
Love bird

Rose-breasted
Cockatoo

Black-headed
Caique

Fig. 1.1 Some of the Parrot Family

PARROT FAMILY UNIQUE

Parrots and parrot–like birds possess features which are unique:

1. Beak which is hinged, the upper mandible being attached to the forehead in a manner which allows great movement and flexibility for cracking seeds and nuts.

2. Lower mandible is light, thin and deep which cuts into the food. It is shorter than the upper, curved mandible.

3. Foot of the parrot is completely zygodactyle (two toes pointing forward and two back and prehensile (capable of grasping) thus allowing great mobility, being able to climb vertical posts or trees, also its beak in the process.

4. The fleshy tongue is thick and muscular and allows the bird to taste food and manipulate it within the beak, discarding husks or pods which are not eaten.

Obviously this summary does not cover the multitude of varieties which exist. Special mention must be made of the Lories and Lorikeets which possess a tongue containing a brush of strong hairs used for procuring nectar food and pollen from flowers.

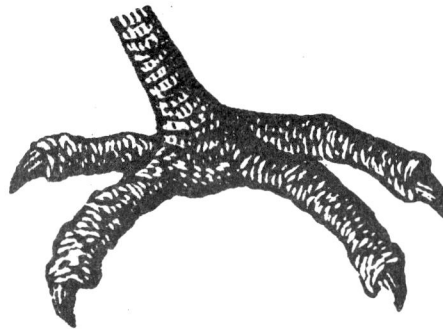

Fig. 1.2 Foot of Parrot–like Bird (2 toes back and front give bird amazing manoeuvrability)

Fig.1.3 Head of Parrot–like Bird

PERIOPHALMIC RING

RED BEAK
UPPER MANDIBLE

LOWER MANDIBLE

MOUSTACHIAL STRIPE
OR MANDIBULAR BANDS

IRIS' IRIDES

BROAD NUCHAL COLLAR

RED SHOULDER PATCH

SECONDARIES

PRIMARIES

TWO FRONT TOES
BACK TOES

LONG TAIL
50% OF FULL LENGTH

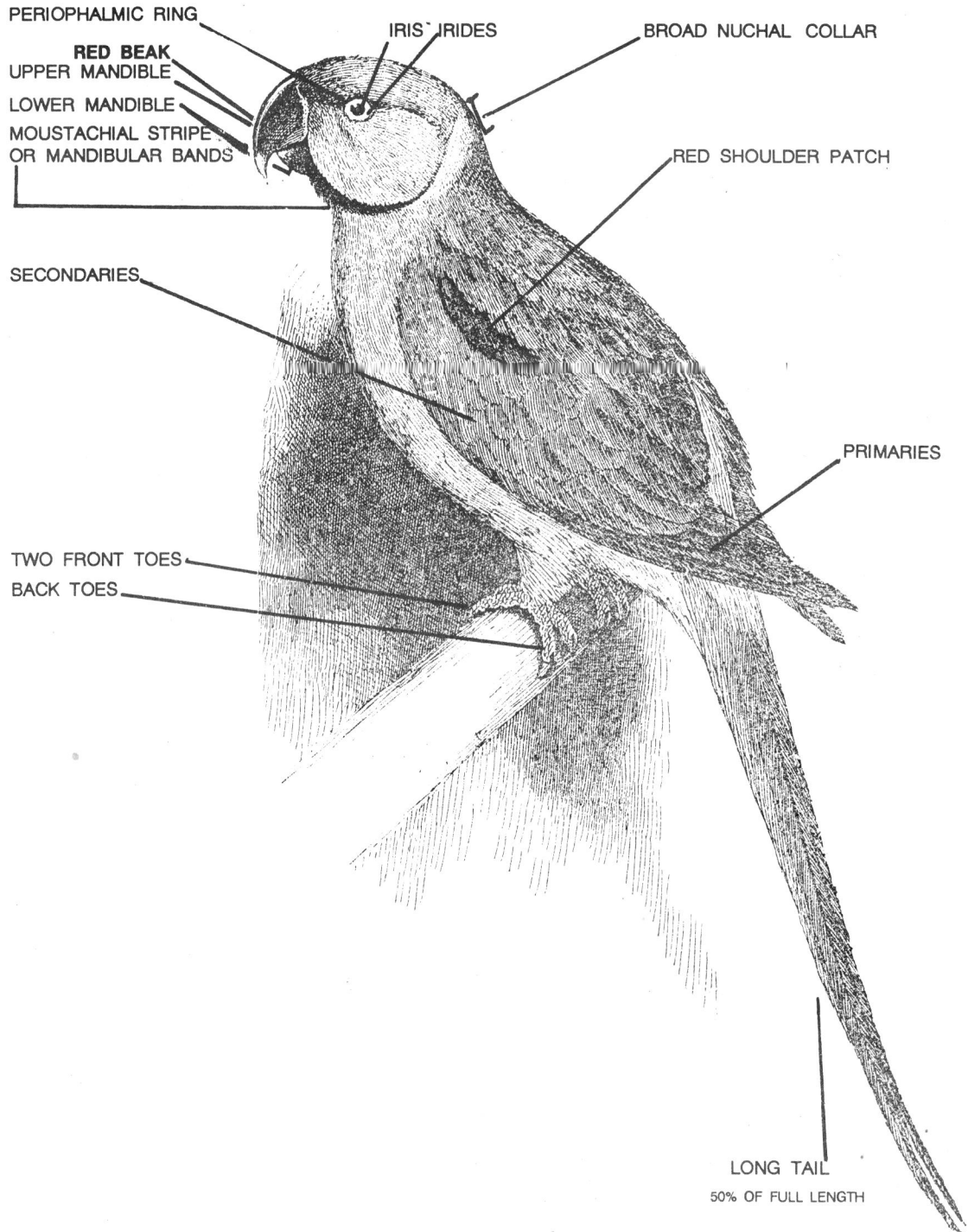

NOTE: Length approx. 20 – 21 Inches
(54cm.) Tail approx.12 Ins.Five species
–vary In size

Fig. 1.4 Features of the Alexandrine (Male)

2

OUTLINE:
THE RINGNECKED PARRAKEETS

A DOMESTICATED SPECIES

Without doubt Ring Necked Parrakeets ("Ring Necks") have one of the longest histories in domestication. It stretches back to the time before Christianity when the Romans kept parrots, the Ring Neck being specifically mentioned (see Chapter 3).

Even in their wild state the Indian Ring-Necked Parrakeet is partly domesticated. It flies in large flocks, raiding orchards and fields in its native India, "Home" is on buildings and in trees and is quite familiar with the noise of people and traffic. Just as pigeons have settled in our towns so have the Parrakeets in India.

Moreover, they have nested in gardens on a regular basis and many delightful accounts have been recorded of their quarrels with other birds and their nesting and feeding habits.

DISTRIBUTION

Ring Necks are to be found in many lands, being kept in cages, aviaries and enclosures. Although there is no record of their being allowed to fly free (homing parrakeets) in the U.K. there is little doubt that they would be suitable subjects in the correct environment. This practice has been followed with Budgerigars and there is no reason why Parrakeets should not be kept in the same way (see *Homing Budgerigars* , Duke of Bedford, Nimrod Press.

Their native haunts are to be found in Africa, and India and it is believed to be the only species to be in existence on two separate continents.

In terms of popularity the Indian bird is undoubtedly a comfortable winner. There is little difference between the two species, but the African species does have a dark red beak.

AFRICAN RING -NECKED

This bird is distributed in various regions of West Africa north of the

Fig. 2.1 Distribution Map :Indian Ring Necks

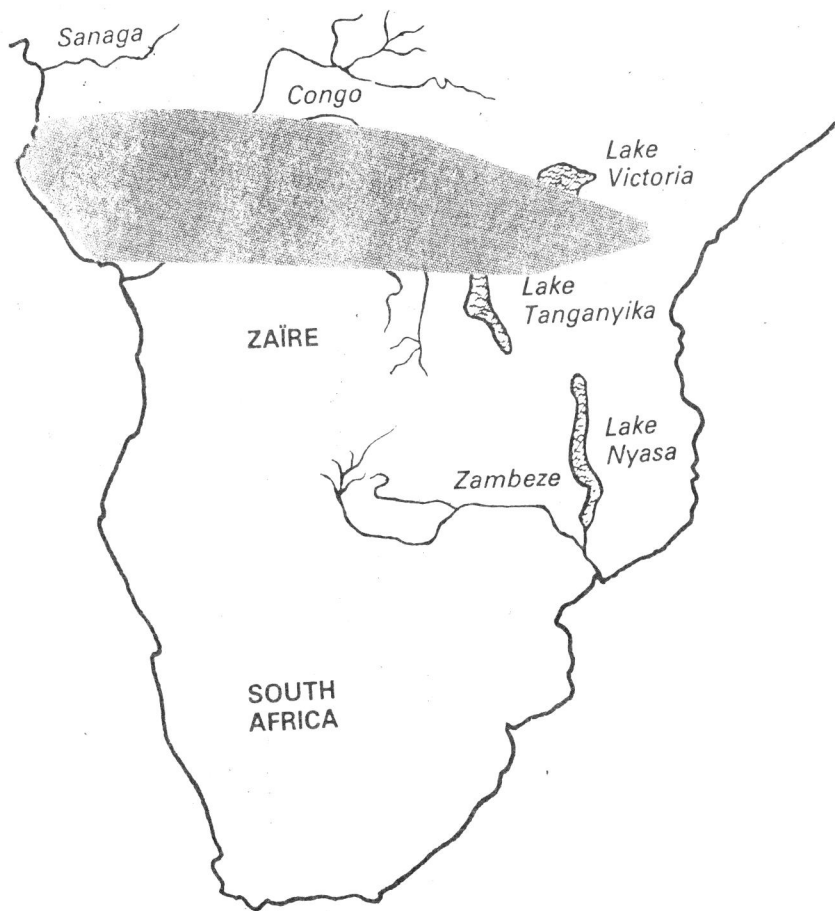

Fig. 2.2 Distribution Map :African Ring Necks

equator, a broad band taking in Senegal, Gambia, Guinea on the West coast and across and southerly to the Sudan and Uganda.

Opinions differ on the exact areas, being obscured by the fact that aviary birds have been released in some areas and then bred in the wild.

The birds inhabit woodlands, cultivated areas and areas which are adjacent to conurbations.

INDIAN RING NECKS

This bird resides in India, Ceylon and Burma.

After breeding is over they fly around in large flocks, generally making a nuisance of themselves. Fruit, corn and generally anything they can find which is edible will be eaten.

ALEXANDRINE PARRAKEET (*Psittacula eupatria*)

A larger Ring-Necked Parrakeet is the Alexandrine, which is around 4 in. (100 mm) longer than the Indian Ring-Necked. This is a beautiful Parrakeet, imperial in bearing and feathering which is fine and silky.

The management is identical to the normal Ring-Neck except the aviary flight should be about a metre longer.

According to the Marquess of Tavistock and Jean Delacour the Alexandrine is more gentle that the Indian or African Ring-Necked Parrakeets. In fact, it is so inoffensive that smaller birds may try to take advantage.

Alternative sources have suggested that Alexandrines can be rather vicious and should not be placed in an aviary with other birds. This appears to be a case of variation amongst individuals so breeders must judge for themselves.The author has found them to be similar to Indian Ring-Necks.

VERSATILITY

Ring Necks are active birds requiring a great deal of room to keep them fit enough for breeding. Some authors have suggested that an aviary 24 ft. in length is essential or cocks will not be fertile. This may be an exaggeration, but certainly as much room as possible is desirable.

Reports of birds performing tricks have been recorded. They vary from ringing bells, threading beads, moving objects and even "counting". In short, Ring Necks are extremely clever. Moreover, handled properly they can be very tame although not as much as some of the larger species.

Ring Necks have been known to talk, but since this implies keeping them in a cage away from other birds, this practice is not really to be encouraged. They are better free-flying in a large aviary enjoying the company of other birds of their own kind.

As discussed later it safer to have one pair per aviary when breeding,but a communal flight is acceptable at other times.

THE MERITS (AND DISADVANTAGES)

Undoubtedly the Ring-Necked Parrakeets have been (and still are the most popular of Parrakeets. They are beautiful, can be made tame, and can be taught simple words which they will repeat to the amusement of all listening. The main disadvantage is the raucous cry, which can be quite irritating and not likely to improve neighbour relationships. When the aviary is approached the birds will fly from one side to another squawking and sometimes, during the process, a vicious hen will attempt to nip the cock who drops his awareness of that danger.

Some breeders do not find the noise unpleasant. It is not constant and neither is it a continuous chatter like, for example, an aviary full of lovebirds.

A NOTE ON TERMINOLOGY

Confusion exists on the names given to Ring-Neck Parrakeets, both in English and in the Scientific names:

ENGLISH NAMES

Indian Ring-Necked Parrakeet
African Ring-Necked Parrakeet
Bengal Parrot
Rose-Ringed Parrakeet

Group Name : Long-Tailed Parrakeets

SCIENTIFIC NAMES: *Psittacula krameri*
*Sub-Species – *Psittacula krameri krameri* (African)
Sub-Species : *Psittacula krameri manillerisis* (Indian)

OBSOLETE NAMES:

Palaeornis torquata (Indian)
P. docilis (African)

OTHER SUB-SPECIES

Other sub-species which exist are:

1. *Psittacula k. parvirostris*
2. *Psittacula k. borealis*

Both are from Asia, but are not seen very often in captivity.

*Some writers classify P.k.krameri as the nomimate race and not as a sub-species

PERSONAL EXPERIENCE WITH THE ALEXANDRINE

Having kept Indian Ring Necks it seemed natural to progress to the Alexandrine a larger, more stately bird with an uncertain reputation. As noted different bird keepers recorded quite opposite views on the behaviour and temperament; one view is that the Alexandrine is a friendly bird who mixes readily with other birds; the other extreme is that he is a boisterous, noisy bird who bullies other birds.

Unfortunately, behaviour is not a simple process. There are many factors which affect the final analysis: age, health, bringing up, housing and fooding. Any factor which brings about uncertainty can result in aggressiveness.

A cock bird six years of age was purchased from a Mrs. Jordan. He is a magnificent bird, fully twenty inches in length, but to make a comparison with an Indian Ring Neck 16 inches in length is quite misleading. It is *not* simply a matter of four inches difference in length.

There is a much greater breadth, longer wings, a massive head and a collar which is larger and wider. It is the Indian Ring Neck on a large scale, but also more stately and elegant.

He had been kept in a cage about 3 ft x 2 ft and, whilst he was quite happy and well cared for, he lacked exercise and missed companionship. Apparently he squawked quite loudly when visitors arrived, but otherwise he was fairly quiet.

The climate was still mild, being the end of the Summer. Accordingly it seemed a good opportunity to acclimatise him to outdoor life. He was placed in an aviary with four Indian Ring Necks and his behaviour observed.

At first he was quite aggressive, regarding all aviary companions as enemies. If a Ring Neck landed near him it was met with a vicious grab from the rather large and strong beak. Fortunately no damage was done; the smaller birds quickly saw the danger and avoided collision.

His inability to fly was an advantage to his companions. He sat on a perch in the far corner of the aviary, but there were other landing spots nearby so the Ring Necks skilfully avoided him.

After about three weeks he seemed to realise that these were his own kind. He gradually mixed with them enjoying their company and squawking whenever approached by humans. His flying abilities improved so the crash dives which were so frequent at first, soon became a thing of the past. Once settled he behaved quite normally .

THE OLDEST FANCIER?

The Alexandrine is said to have been named after Alexander the Great who was the eighteenth King of Macedon (356 BC – 323 BC). This remarkable man, scholar, soldier, conqueror and ruler is thought to have been the first to keep Parrots, these being Ring Neck Parrakeets. As noted in Chapter 3 Alexander brought these birds from India to Greece. They were then taken up by the Romans and subsequently spread throughout the world as cage or aviary birds.

NOTE: Features
as for Alexandrine
,but no Shoulder
patches.Smaller in
overall size (25%
smalier)

Fig. 2.3 Features of Ring-Necked Parrakeet

Fig. 2.4 Natural Habitat of Ring-Necks

3

HISTORY OF THE RING-NECKED PARRAKEETS

ANCIENT HISTORY

The ancient history of parrots and parrakeets is very relevant to a study of the Ring-Necked Parrakeet because, according to early writers, whenever reference is made in ancient writing to parrots, the Ring Neck Parrakeet is the one that is always meant. As noted by eminent authors :

RING-NECKED PARRAKEET , INDIA

The ROSE-RINGED PARRAKEET (Palaornis docilis*), WEST AFRICA , Psittacus torquatus* (Russ), Psittacus Alexandri, Psittacus manillensis, Psittacus docilis. English dealers' name – Ring-necked Parrakeet. German name ' "Kleiner Alexandersittich"

These are practically the same birds. This Parrot is the only species indigenous to both Africa and Asia, and, as mentioned in the introductory remarks, the Rose-ringed Parrakeet is the Parrot which the Romans brought from Africa in Nero's time, and which is mentioned in the writings of Aristotle, and described by Pliny. The only difference between the Indian and African Ring-necked Parrakeet is that the former have red and the latter black beaks.

In Calcutta and in Ceylon these Parrakeets are found wild in every garden, and , tame specimens are so common throughout India , that sailors bring them over on almost every ship coming home from the East. No other Parrot is more docile, and though slow to learn to talk, the Ring-necked Parrakeet acquires a very clear pronunciation.

When first imported, care is requisite to avoid colds, but with judicious treatment they become very hardy, and will live many years on a mixture of all kinds of seeds. The female and young birds have no ring round the neck.

* The Old Name:this historical reference is in the original version .

GENERAL HISTORY

As noted Ring-Necked Parrakeets are the first to be mentioned in literature on Parrots. It is for that reason that a synopsis of the history of the Parrot family is now reproduced:

The docility of the Parrots, the facility with which most kinds can be accustomed to cage-life, and the talent of some species for imitating the human voice and pronouncing words or sentences, have made Parrots favourite cage-birds, and sufficiently explain that, when America was first discovered, they were found domesticated by the natives, and that tame Parrots have been kept as pets by the natives of India from time immemorial.

According to Dr. Finsch, Parrots were unknown to the ancient Israelites. The earliest mention of Parrots to be found in ancient history occurs in the description of a festival which took place in Alexandria, in Egypt, 284 B.C. In the time of Alexander the Great the first Parrots were brought to Greece by a General returning from India. But Aristotle, classing the Psittacea with the birds of prey, evidently never saw a Parrot, and derived his scant information from hearsay. Fifty years before Christ, Parrots were known to the Romans, for Parrots are mentioned in writings of that date as brought from Syria. Pliny, A.D. 50, gave the first description of some Parrots found by the emissaries of the Emperor Nero on the banks of the Nile, and evidently Palaeornis torquatus, or the Ring-necked Parrakeet, is meant. Other early writers mention India as the Native country of Parrots, and say that the birds were not eaten in India, but were held sacred on account of their ability to imitate the human voice.

In Rome, Parrots became articles of luxury at an early date, and the price of a Parrot often exceeded that of a slave. During the feasts of the Emperor Antonius Heliogabalus, dishes of cooked Parrot-heads were served, and the same Emperor's lions were sometimes fed with Peacocks and Parrots.

It is nearly certain that the Romans knew no other kind than the Ring-necked Parrakeet. From the first century of the Christian era, history is almost silent on the subject of Parrots during 1,400 years. The Eastern trade had come into the hands of the Venetians and of the Portuguese, and Parrots appear not to have been transported by the tedious trade routes of the Middle Ages. In 1455 a Senegal Parrot was first heard of in Europe. Towards the end of the fifteenth century (1498) the Portuguese circumnavigated the Cape, and acquired during the next years a part of India, where tame Parrots were found by them in many houses of natives.

Columbus, too, had returned from his voyage of discovery to America, and had brought Parrots with him when he held his solemn entry in Seville on March 31, 1493. In England the first Parrots were shown as a great curiosity in 1504. A book of birds published in Zurich in 1557 mentions fourteen kinds of Parrots, of which seven can be now recognised by the description published 345 years ago. As a curiosity it may be mentioned that in 1707 a description and illustration of the Great Black Cockatoo of New Guinea was published at Amsterdam, whilst up to the present day this bird is so rare that a live specimen sells in London at a very high price.

From 1747 to 1764 "A Natural History of Uncommon Birds", by Edwards, was published in London, which depicted 37 species of Parrots; Brisson's "Ornithologia", published 1760, more than doubled the number of known Parrots, and Latham's "General Synopsis of Birds" (1781) added 45 new Parrots to those described by the former author, 25 of these new species being Parrots from Australia and the South Sea Islands.

Buffon's "Natural History of Birds" (Paris, 1783) contains drawings of 82 species of Parrots. Shaw, in the "Zoology of New Holland" (1794), first mentions the Undulated Parrakeet, or Budgerigar, of which many thousands are now imported annually into Europe. In the beginning of this century about 120 varieties of Parrots were known. Wagler's work on Parrots, published in Munich, 1832, contained a description of nearly 200 varieties of the Parrot family, which number had grown to 350 by 1867, when Dr. Finsch published his exhaustive monograph on Parrots. Of these 350 Parrots, 142 species are indigenous to America, 23 to Africa, 18 to Asia, 83 to the Moluccas, 59 to Australia, and 29 to Polynesia.

Not a single species of Parrot is, or ever has been, indigenous to Europe. In view of the distribution of Parrots over the warm and temperate zones of all the rest of the world, the absence of Parrots from Europe is curious. The climate alone cannot be the cause, for we find in North America the Carolina Parrakeet as far north as 430 northern latitude, and in Polynesia we find the New Zealand Parrakeet as far south as 550 southern latitude on the Himalayas, Parrots are found 4,000 feet above sea-level, and on the Andes close to the snow region. It is abundantly proved that very many Parrots would thrive perfectly well in our climate. Some years since, the owner of an estate in England practically tried to acclimatise Parrots by turning out a number of Cockatoos and other, mostly Australian Parrots. The experiment succeeded beyond expectation, as far as the climate was concerned but it seems few men with a gun in their hands can see a strange bird without shooting it, and the expensive Parrots let loose by an enthusiastic ornithologist were all wantonly shot.

In size the Parrots vary from that of a Linnet to that of the well-known Macaw and large Cockatoo. Their intelligence and docility vary as much as their size. The best talkers are the African Grey Parrots, and next to them the Brazilian Amazons, the Cockatoo from the Moluccas, and the Indian Ring-necked Parrakeet. Australian Parrots do not as readily learn to talk, but please the eye by their brilliant plumage.

No other birds become so entirely domesticated and so much attached to their keepers as Parrots, and none are so long-lived. But many Parrots utter distracting screams, which may become quite unbearable. It is well to know, however, that most Parrots only scream from fear, and quite forget this bad habit when they become thoroughly tame. Their powerful beaks render Parrots very destructive, and their keeper should therefore provide the strongest possible cages. Experience shows that the larger Parrots, and especially the tame ones, thrive best when kept singly in cages. Tame Parrots are extremely jealous, and to place these in an aviary* will cause them often to pine, or to become exceedingly quarrelsome; in the latter case they will inflict fearful

*Obviously no longer a view held.

injury on each other. Almost all Parrots possess very much individuality, and form strong attachments and equally strong antipathies.

ACCOMMODATION FOR PARRAKEETS

From early times Parrakeets have been kept in cages because it was thought they were much happier when confined within a house or other building. Certainly a suitable cage is better than a chain affixed to the leg, but, as shown by modern researchers, close confinement can lead to serious problems including feather picking.

A writer of a hundred years ago had the following remarks to make:

The best cage to keep these parrakeets in, as they are rather powerful birds, is the ordinary parrot cage, square pattern, which must be fitted with a smallish perch, as the grasping powers of the toes are not sufficiently good to enable the bird to clutch its foot round the ordinary sized perch fitted to these cages. The food vessels must be inside the cage, and made to revolve outwards whenever it becomes necessary to replenish them. Water must be provided for these birds, both in the shape of a constant supply for drinking purposes and a daily bath; few of the family of parrakeets are so fond of bathing as this species. Many people who keep parrots or parrakeets have an idea that they can live without water, and treat their birds in accordance with this belief. This ought not to be the case; the idea is not only absurd but cruel, and opposed to common sense. We wonder how their owners would like to be treated like the birds are. Water is just as necessary for parrots and parrakeets as it is for any other living creature, and to deprive them of it is opposed to all dictates of nature.

They ought not to have either milk, sop, or meat, because if they do they will in all probability develop the disfiguring habit of feather-plucking, which causes the bird to have a most unsightly appearance. It generally plucks or nibbles all the feathers within reach of its beak, and a bird that has gnawed all the feathers off its body and legs, leaving those of its head alone for the sole reason that it cannot get at them, is a most unpleasant object to look upon. Once a parrot has formed this wretched habit it is a most difficult task to break him of it; indeed, in nine cases out of ten the habit is never eradicated. All sorts of dodges have been tried; cardboard rings have been made to put round the bird's neck sufficiently wide to prevent him, or her, as the case may be, getting at his feathers to nibble them, but in many cases this is a useless proceeding, as "Polly" simply tears the ring to pieces with his feet and then starts the habit once more. The only thing that we have found effectual, and then only in some cases, is to supply "Parrish's Chemical Food" in its drinking water, but, fortunately, we very rarely have examples that want treating for this complaint, as we never allow our parrots to have animal food of any kind.

The plainer the food the better the birds will thrive, and such seeds as canary, hemp, millet, oats, maize, and barley are all that our bird get, with the exception of a little "tit-bit" in the shape of a small piece of carrot or potato. This dietary and water ad. lib. will keep any parrot in the best of health and spirits, and a medicine chest will be an ornament and not a necessity to the bird room.

AVIARIES AND BIRD ROOMS

Fortunately for the Parrakeet and all parrots generally there is now full recognition given to the fact that home bred birds are desirable and, to be able to breed, extensive aviaries should be provided. Ideally an aviary of around 3 metres long and 2 metres wide should be the aim with a height of 2 metres*. This allows the birds full scope for exercise and keeping fit – so vital for captive breeding.

Serious aviculturists keep birds to breed with them so obviously they aim to simulate conditions similar to those found in the wild.

Like many changes they come slowly until they become a natural process, rather than the exception. The fact remains that there is now general acceptance of the need for adequate aviaries designed for each species, after considering the desirable features. Many breeders have been responsible together with the Avicultural Society, the Parrot Society and other bodies. Two names worthy of mention as pioneers in scientific breeding are:

1. The Marquess of Tavistock
2. E.J. Boosey

Their experiences were recorded in the "Avicultural Magazine" and "The Foreigner" more than 50 years ago. The record by Mr. Boosey is of a general nature, whereas the Marquess of Tavistock gives a more detailed description over a period. The trials and tribulations experienced should serve as a reminder to would-be bird keepers that chicks should definitely not be count-ed before hatched – or even after they have emerged from the eggs!

THE BREEDING OF LUTINO RING-NECKS
By The Marquess of Tavistock

This article might also be called *Per ardua ad astra* since it must be about eighteen years ago that Mr. Ezra gave me a lovely golden parr-akeet with red eyes and white flight feathers and I embarked on the thorny path of endeavour in trying to get her to reproduce her virtues in her descendants. This original bird (she is still alive but has not bred for many years and is obviously aged) though a wonderful colour, was not otherwise a good speci-men, having a rather humped-up look and flying heavily, and these def-ects she unfortunately transmitted to her offspring with unnecessary fidelity.

I knew little about parrakeet breeding in those days and kept her and her green mate in an indoor bird-room with the not unnatural result of clear eggs for two successive seasons. I then tried her in a small fixed outdoor aviary and

*A long flight is essential for breeding and height to simulate tree dwelling conditions

my stock was added to by a further generous gift by Mr. Ezra of a really fine hen, perfect not only in colour but in every other respect.

From these birds , during the next few years, I succeeded in raising about seven or eight green young ones, but only one, a hen, was a really good specimen, the others being under-sized or defective in their wings and flying badly. The only surviving child of the best hen was a small cock, not too good in his wings, and with a permanently moth-eaten look round his neck. As long as they remained in their original quarters I could not, moreover, get a fertile egg from any of the males I bred.

Then came the transfer of the stock to the 24 ft. movable aviaries* I still use. A decided improvement followed. The first year, from the two lutino hens mated to green wild cocks, I reared four much better young ones. One of these unfortunately died while under the temporary care of a friend: the other three, two nice cocks and a moderate hen, I still have.

The lutino-bred greens being, with one exception, still in immature plumage , and difficult to sex, I turned all together into the same aviary. Two hens nested and one hatched her egg, but the young one I found dead a day or two later with its beak and toes bitten off. I attributed the misdeed to a vicious spinster hen and to colony breeding, but I learned later who was the real culprit.

Next year I paired the best lutino hen to a fair-sized ,but badly-shaped lutino-bred cock ,and the old hen to the rough-necked cock. Both duly went to nest and this time both lots of eggs were fertile and my hopes of lutinos began to run high. One morning, half-way through the incubation period, I noticed the mate of the best hen looking ill and caged him in the hospital. A few hours later the lutino was off and also looking ill so I had to cage her and give the eggs to an unmated Alexandrine Parrakeet who was incubating an infertile clutch. By evening the lutino-bred cock was dead; by next morning his mate was dead. So sudden had been their illness that I felt sure they had picked up rat poison but a post-mortem examination revealed a virulent form of pneumonia. In due course the Alexandrine hatched the orphan eggs and immediately killed the young ones. She had incubated infertile clutches so long that I believe she regarded it as a shocking and unnatural event that eggs should produce tiny pink monstrosities and did her best to hush up the unpleasant affair.

About the same time the old lutino was due to hatch and I looked into the nest. Another tragedy: Tiny mangled corpses minus beaks and feet. I knew that the hen was a good mother and would not be guilty of this outrage so the blame must fall on her disreputable husband with the ragged neck. He doubtless had murdered his former offspring by the lutino-bred hen the previous season. The next year I put the ragged cock with the only really good lutino-bred hen I had reared in the fixed aviaries, intending to remove him before the eggs hatched and run him with the lutino hen, also for a limited period. The lutino-bred duly vanished into her nest-box. (To give the cock his due he is an attentive husband to any lady of his race whatever his sins may be as a parent.) After a time when I judged it wise to change the cock I looked into the nest. No eggs, no hen. I hunted everywhere for a corpse and found nothing.

*Movable now appear out of favour , ,but for those with space are to be recommended.

She had vanished into thin air and to this day I do not know what became of her.

I tried the rough-necked cock with the lutino hen for several more years but had no luck. Sometimes the young were dead in the shell. Sometimes they died soon after hatching, in some cases through my fault for I put the nest in the shelter instead of in the open flight. Finally, the old lady started having trouble with egg-binding. Then she missed a season with a catarrhal discharge from one nostril, and after that she stopped laying, though every spring she retired into her nest and for weeks and weeks spent a soothing time of retreat incubating the memories of the past – a habit I find very common with ancient dames of her genus.

I was now left with two cocks and a hen lutino-bred green reared in movable aviaries and two hens bred in fixed aviaries, one a big bird but a poor flier, the other small and also a poor flier. The small hen I sometimes tried with the rough-necked cock, but she was terribly clumsy with her eggs and year after year contrived to crack or dent any that were fertile, losing the only young she happened to hatch.

The big hen laid two eggs in a nest in the shelter. Both hatched, and to my delight one was a lutino. Alas: the situation was all against the health of the young. Both left the nest hopelessly rickety and died a few days later.

Next year I gave her a grandfather-clock nest outside, and she damaged both her eggs. The other pair with a similar nest lost their young one as soon as it hatched. All three hens appeared to be firm believers in birth-control, never laying more than two eggs in a year and often only one.

Next came the moving of the birds to Peasmarch. The hen bred in a movable aviary was upset by the change and did not nest at all. The big hen again hatched two young ones, a lutino and a green. Both were fine birds but within a few days of leaving the next the lutino died of sunstroke: The same season the small hen mated to the rough-necked cock managed single-handed to rear a nice green young one, a far better specimen than either of its parents. It and the nest-mate of the dead lutino are still alive and are both males. They are strong and robust birds.

Last year the mother of the lutino had two green young ones. One died in the nest when half-grown. The other, a cock, was reared but was a poor specimen and I gave it away when a year old.

The movable aviary pair reared a lutino and a green to leave the nest, the former a very nice one. The green hurt itself and died a few days after flying and soon afterwards the lutino was found paralysed in both legs. With careful nursing it seemed likely to recover, but it finished by regaining complete use of one foot only and I had to give it away as a pet. The small hen again damaged her eggs.

Next year came round with hopes not inconsiderably chastened by former experiences. All three hens took to their nests. When the incubation period was up I looked in the nest of the one that bred the first lutino. Nothing, not even eggs: She must be nearly sixteen years old and had her toes badly frost-bitten some winters ago so probably, never having being a good bird, her breeding days are done. The small hen had one addled egg and one with a dead chick with the usual dent in the shell.

The third pair had two young but both were green. These were reared and are fair specimens. Once more, it seemed, I must wait for the coming of another season with my stock reduced by a hen no longer breeding; but the unexpected happened. For the first time in her life the small hen laid again: Her mate was duly removed when hatching drew near and, amazing to relate, she hatched both her eggs. Still more amazing both young birds proved to be lutinos and fine specimens at that. They are now out of the nest and flying strongly. Though I could wish she were more skilful in the handling of her eggs, I have nothing but praise for the devotion of the scrubby little green mother. So poor a flier that she gets about entirely by climbing, late in the season and single-handed, she has done her offspring so well that they look as though they had been reared by wild Ringnecks of the best quality. But it will not do to rely on appearances too far; if they live to reach breeding age I shall mate them to strong wild greens and thus try and eliminate any faults, constitutional or moral, that may have come down to them from their dubious ancestry.

The results of this somewhat protracted experiment indicate that every pair of lutino-bred greens should produce a percentage of lutinos if mated *interse.* * Probably this rule holds good with the breeding of all rare colour varieties of Parrakeets. For some reason or other it is usually, in practice, wise to get all the young you can from your rare-coloured bird mated to normal wild ones and pair the progeny *interse* and NOT to break your original pair in order to mate son to mother or father to daughter; the result of the latter venture is apt to be infertile eggs and wasted seasons.

Of the young Ringnecks from lutino-bred parents that have lived long enough for their colour to be discernible, eight have been green and five lutino, which is, I think, very near the Mendelian percentage.

HOW TO BREED RING-NECKED PARRAKEETS*
By E.J.Boosey

The Ring-neck is an attractively coloured bird, being mainly a beautiful apple-green with a darker green, long, tapering tail washed with blue, and a black ring on the lower part of the cheek, starting from the base of the lower mandible, but not quite joining another ring of bright pink which starts from the back of the neck. The face colour is considerably more vivid than that of the rest of the body and the back of the head is tinged with blue.

Hens are completely green, the colour having, if anything, a more yellowish tinge than the cocks and they entirely lack the ring round the neck.

African Species

There is also an African race of the Ring-neck (*P sittacula krameri*) which only differs from its Indian relative by being slightly smaller and having a rather brownish beak.

Ring-necks make admirable aviary birds, being extremely hardy and perfectly simple both to keep and breed. Being rather large birds – from 16 to 17 inches in length – they naturally cannot be expected to do well for long in a

*Amongst themselves. This is interesting , not complying with the normal practice of inbreeding to fix a characteristic

small fixed aviary, but provided they can be given a movable aviary measuring about 20 ft. long over all and not necessarily more than 4 ft. wide, they will flourish and be no trouble at all to their owner.

Most of the Parrakeets of this genus evince a desire to go to nest somewhat inconveniently early, though provided the hen does not get egg-bound in the cold weather, there is little harm in allowing them to do so as the young are not delicate in the nest when first hatched, as are, for instance, Many-colours.

They often want to breed as early as February, but as they are only single-brooded, it is really just as well to keep them waiting for their nest box until at least the middle of March.

They should be given the usual grandfather clock nest stood in the open run, and when the young ones are hatched the parents will be found to consume large quantities of apple, monkey-nuts and hemp. No extras, however, of any kind are necessary though some pairs appreciate spinach-beet. Ring-necks may, therefore, be considered the hardiest and most easily bred Parrakeet that I have yet described in *The Foreigner*.

COURTSHIP DISPLAY AND FEEDING

The cock's courting display is the most amazing performance, as, with blazing eyes and slightly spread wings he hops, bows and squirms round the lady of his choice, giving vent all the time to a curious and not unpleasant sort of song.

His method, too, of feeding his sitting wife when she comes off for exercise, is most amusing. Standing bolt upright at her side he paws the air three times with the foot nearest to her and then proceeds to feed her. This goes on until she thinks she has had enough; and the whole perform-ance to watch is exactly as if the cock were saying "one, two, three, go" in order that his wife shall be ready to receive each mouthful of food at exactly the right moment.

Young Ring-necks stay in the nest rather a long time, and usually look very immaculate when they emerge, though at that period their tails are less long and tapering than those of their parents.

Fortunately, most of the Parrakeets belonging to this family do not need the same close watching the moment their young ones are able to fend for themselves, as is necessary with broadtails, as the former are generally single-brooded, Ring-necks being usually prepared to put up with the presence of their young ones long after they are able to find their own living. If they do eventually have to be removed, it is usually because the hen, and not the cock, has started to object to them. In fact, a hen Ring-neck is a very much less amiable individual than her husband, and though she sub-mits to him during the breeding season, she is usually " king of the castle" at other times of the year, and is often inclined to be quite snappy with her husband.

Ring-necks make the most delightful pets and often learn to talk well. They are extremely intelligent, and some can be taught all kinds of tricks, such as threading beads on a piece of cotton with their beaks, twirling a miniat -ure rod round their heads, and even retrieving a particular card from a row, the bird in this case walking along in front of the cards and picking out the one he reaches when he notices his master's thumb, which is resting on the table, give a slight twitch. Such wonderful talented specimen are, of course, extremely rare, and have usually been trained originally by natives in India.

Tame Ring-necks are fond of sitting on one's hand and climbing about one's body, but usually they have not the African Grey Parrot's fondness for having their heads scratched. The best tame specimens are those which have been hand-reared from the nest, but, unfortunately, at this early stage it is impossible to sex them, otherwise one would take particular care to pick out a cock, as they usually make far more talented talkers and are much more gentle and affectionate than hens.

I once possessed a marvellously tame cock Alexandrine Parrakeet, a species which is exactly like a Ring-neck, and comes from India, but is about 20 instead of 16 inches long.

This bird was in a friend's possession when I went to stay with him, and it had the reputation of being a bit of a mysogonist. For some reason, however, though I was a complete stranger, the Alexandrine decided that he approved of me, and came out at once on to my arm. My friend said nothing at the time, but great was my delight when, two days after I got home, a large wooden box arrived, and when I opened it out came the Alexandrine.

From that time on he was a most devoted companion, being allowed complete liberty in the garden and always roosting in some large yews, which were the nearest trees to my bedroom window. The moment my curtains were drawn in the morning he would fly on to the open casement window, and very often right inside, though I had to discourage this, as he had such an enormously strong beak and was rather inclined to playfully pull my wardrobe to pieces while I was dressing. When I went down to breakfast he never attempted to come with me through the house, but flew straight round to a large tree near the dining-room window.

If I was sitting in the garden he would always find me sooner or later and come down on to the seat. If I was walking in the woods he would fly from tree to tree above me, following me about just as faithfully as any dog.

He once gave the most remarkable proof of his affection that I have seen in any bird. I had bought him a hen who was, even for a hen of this genus, a rather wild and savage ;bird, and spent most of her time inside an old decayed walnut tree. the cock was quite pleased with her, and the two used to fly about together when I was away from home or at any rate not visible in the garden.

They were fed in a special trap feeder which excluded sparrows, and was placed on top of an aviary, and one day as I was replenishing the seed the hen suddenly took it into her head to fly at my hand, but before she could reach it, the cock intercepted her like a shot from a gun, and knocked her clean off the aviary.

A few years later my old home was sold and we went to live in a flat in London. I could, I suppose, have taken the Alexandrine with me, but I dislike keeping the larger parrakeets permanently in cages, and so the two birds were sent to an owner who could give them full liberty in Hampshire. I was terribly sorry to part with the Alexandrine, and even sorrier to hear a few months later that some idiot with a gun had shot him, presumably in mistake for a hawk.

There is a very beautiful golden-yellow edition of the common Ring-neck, these birds being known as lutinos, and having fine, dark, ruby red eyes. A blue variety is also known; in fact, there are actually at the present time blue specimens in captivity, at any rate, in India.

A lutino mated to a normal bird naturally produces normal green young ones, but lutinos have been bred from such young ones when mated brother to sister, or again when one of them is mated to its yellow parent, and the same, of course, would apply to the blue variety.

A really large breeding stock of yellow or blue Ring-necks is a fascinating possibility to contemplate, but actually to breed up such stock is a very long and often heart-breaking business, since the original stock birds themselves are so extremely hard to obtain, and any losses, therefore, so difficult to replace.

REFERENCES

1. The Illustrated Book of Canaries and Cage Birds, Blakston, Swaysland and Weiner, Cassell & Co., London ,1890
2. Cage and Chamber Birds, Beckstein, J.M., Geo Bell, London, 1875
3. The Birds of Southern India, H.R. Baker and Chas. M. Inglis, Madras, India, 1930
4. The Parrots of the World, Forshaw and Cooper, Lansdowne, 1973

Fig. 3.1 Hen Ring -Neck in Flight

4

NATURAL HISTORY

PARRAKEETS IN INDIA

An excellent summary of the Parrakeet in India has been given in a special study of birds by local residents:

Psittacula krameri manillensis (Bechst).

THE ROSE-RINGED PAROQUET*

(Fauna of British India, 2nd edition, No. 1500)
(Fauna of British India, lst edition, No. 1138 (part).)

Description – **Male** : Length about l6.5"; wing 6.75"; tail 9 to 9.5"; bill at gape ".

Upper mandible cherry-red with a black tip; lower mandible horny brown.

Head and face emerald-green; a narrow black line from nostrils to eyes ; nape and hind neck tinged lilac. A demi-ring round the back of neck the colour of "sunset" roses, it can hardly I think be called pink as it has a decided tinge of orange in it; back and scapulars green; rump and upper tail-coverts emerald-green; primary coverts green washed with blue; primaries and secondaries dark green margined with light yellow and a portion of their inner webs dusky. Central tail-feathers blue, remainder blue on the outer webs, yellowish-green on the inner, all with dark brown shafts. The lower aspect of all tail-feathers greenish-yellow. From the chin down the neck and forming a demi-collar, black; remainder of lower plumage yellowish-green.

Female : Similar to male, but without the rose and black collars; in the place of which she has a narrow emerald-green collar.

Locality, habits, etc. One of the commonest Indian Paroquets and at the same time pehaps the most destructive; it associates in large flocks and frequents cultivated areas, gardens, etc., being particularly in evidence when the corn fields are ripening; it then swarms down upon the fields morning and evening, and each bird, if not disturbed, will deliberately nip off and carry away a head of corn. It also does immense damage to fruit, as we know to our own cost, especially to guava-trees, littering the ground below with half-eaten fruit.

Breeding season February or March.

* Note: the original spelling of Parrakeet has been left.

Nest It nests in holes of trees of of buildings and walls, under the roof of houses, etc.

Eggs 4; white; average measurement 1.2 x .95"

From all accounts the position remains the same today, the Ring Necks being very plentiful and displaying the same habits. If anything the range of places where they are found is now extended.

THE RING-NECKED PARRAKEET IN MY GARDEN*

The garden from which I write is in Larkana, in Upper Sind, and it is full of trees. Some of these trees are old and have holes in the trunks and branches and already pairs of Ring-necked Parrakeets can be seen clinging to the outside bark and discussing nesting sites. The garden seems full of Parrakeets, and at almost any time of the day their voices can be heard in some part of the garden; either they are flying swiftly and calling as they fly, or they sit in the shade among the leaves, chattering to or among themselves.

Though very common in India and a curse to the cultivator, whose crops they constantly despoil, they are very lovely birds, particularly in the early morning before the light is too harsh and bright and the soft velvety smoothness of their plumage shows at its best. How at the end of January it is cold in the mornings, and from 8 to 9 o'clock the Parrakeets sun themselves, perching upon the dead branches of trees or upon any branch which stands out exposed to the light. One can stand beneath the branches and look up and see the bright beady eye, the shining red upper mandible, so like a ripe red chilli, one of their favourite foods, and the lovely pink and black ring round the neck of the male and the long and elegant tail, and the feathers upon the head and breast, as smooth as a dove. And one sees them as one rides in the morning along the dusty country roads, if roads these sandy cart tracks can be called, feeding upon grain which has fallen from the laden carts, paddy or rice in the husk, and in its season, corn. As the birds fly up at one's approach, one sees the full beauty of the male, the lovely green, the swift flight, the long and slender tail.

And when taken young from the nest they make most charming pets. In this part of India young are generally available in March, though in South India they nest earlier, in January or February, and basketfuls of half-fledged young can be seen in the bird market in Bombay. One rupee would be a very good price for a fledgling Ring-necked, and eight annas more for a fledgling Alexandrine, the so called "Hill-Parrot" of the Indians, because it comes from the hilly country in the west and central India, with the distinguishing red mark upon the wing. Both the Ring-necked and Alexandrine are the easiest things to rear upon a simple paste of parched grain flour mixed with water to the consistency of putty. If little bits of this can be broken off, rolled into a pellet between finger and thumb, and then put into the fledgling's beak, the young of both Ring-necks and Alexandrines will thrive upon this simple diet.

* Godfrey Davis writing some 50 years ago

into a pellet between finger and thumb, and then put into the fledgling's beak, the young of both Ring-necks and Alexandrines will thrive upon this simple diet. And when I read in the press of young Australian Parrakeets being fed upon a chewed-up mixture of brown bread and apple (and is there raw egg too?), I wonder whether a plain diet of parched or toasted grain flour and water would not do. But fledgling Malabar Parrakeets will not thrive on this. I once lost two out of three on this diet, though the third I saved and it grew into a lovely bird, on a simple diet on which Dr. Amsler fed with such success his Blue Mountain Lorikeets, ground rice, milk, and honey sugar, made as rice mould is made for the table, and about which he once wrote in the Magazine years ago.

Though it may be necessary to keep Ring-neck in large aviaries if they are to breed, they do keep in beautiful condition in comparatively small wire cages. For instance, only the other day upon a station platform, I saw a cock Ring-neck in lovely plumage and very tame and friendly in a strong wire cage with rounded top, not more than a foot in diameter and eighteen inches high, at least that is what I judged it without measurement. But it was not one of the small dome-shaped cages made of hoop iron with a sheet-iron floor, which one sees, alas, so often hanging in the bazaars, but a cage of strong galvanized wire with a clip-on bottom, after the style of the Chinese bird cage. Probably also the owner let the bird out of its cage, as tame Parrakeets commonly are.

When the young fledgling can feed itself it is still fed largely on grain, but the grain is not roasted or parched as when it is to be made into flour. The grain, which is a sort of pea, is soaked overnight in water, and fed in the morning to the birds; they are also often given fresh fruit, guava, and mango in season, ripe red chillies and green vegetables, such as Wali-sang, a sort of country scarlet runner, and indeed the wild flocks play havoc in the vegetable gardens and orchards. Particularly do the birds love the half-ripe mangoes when they are of the consistency of an apple three-quarters ripe. I have often thought how hard it is for Parrots to be fed largely on hard seed, seeing how small a part hard seeds must fill in the dietary of a wild Parrot throughout the year. When no cultivated crops or fruits are available the Ring-neck feeds upon wild fruits or seeds, the wild fig or the seeds within the husks of the tali tree. They are purely vegetarians, and fresh vegetarians at that, for choice they and also drink something stronger than water when they can get it.

They join the noisy throng of Mynas and Rosy Pastors and Bulbuls and Sunbirds on the silk cotton trees when in February the lovely scarlet flowers appear and offer free drinks of nectar to the birds. In captivity, or perhaps I should say domestication (because the Ring-neck is ,essentially, a pet and should be made much of, and not kept, captive, in a cage), the Ring-neck when hand-reared, as he should be, is both affectionate sometimes, when he not only postures, as he does to his wild mate on a branch of a tree, but regurgitates his food. Above all, he is a bird that can be kept with a good conscience, for while ever so much good can be said of him when he is wild, and it is a pity that an ordered and supervised transport cannot make him more easily available to bird lovers at home.

I shall miss him when I retire, though I like to think I shall be able to keep and breed a pair in an orchard in England; and Mynas and Doves and Bulbuls and Grey Partridges and lots of other birds. How rarely do dreams come true.

EVERYDAY LIFE

An excellent description of the everyday life of the "Green Parrakeet" is to be found in *Birds in my Indian Garden* by Malcolm MacDonald, Jonathan Cape, London, 1960. There are also excellent monochrome photographs by Christina Loke.

In the wild, as in captivity, the birds nest early in the year. A hole in a suitable tree is the usual site. If necessary the female will excavate further, spending days on getting the cavity large enough. In this labouring the cock bird is an observer leaving all the hard work to his companion.

The preparation may take many months of the preceding year, the pair staying together during the day to hunt for food. The reserving of the nest is a preliminary to the process of mating, egg laying and rearing which is to follow.

Early in February the cock shows more interest in the hen and will probably mate with her. After showing his intentions by moving around her and caressing with his beak he mounts her back, gripping the back of the head, while she crouches down to support the action of the coition. This is not a simple matter and the long tails may make contact quite difficult.

After the first mating others followed and the birds went through a period of courtship; indeed frantic activity went on for about a fortnight.

Each night the hen went on the nest and the next morning there was copulation and the cock fed the hen by regurgitation. After exercise the hen would return to the nest.

The mating was observed and recorded and it was found that the love making extended to l8th March, a period of almost 7 weeks. From that time the hen concentrated on sitting and towards the end of March she appeared agitated and it appeared that possibly chicks had hatched.

During this period the hen incubated the eggs and the cock fed her. This feeding by regurgitation continued after the chicks were hatched.

For about a month after hatching the cock fed the female. Thereafter she was fed by him, but also went for her own food.

On 7th May the first young Parrakeet looked out of the nest tunnel. It continued to be fed for 3 weeks and then emerged from the nest to fly away. Sadly after all the effort only one youngster emerged.

Once the breeding season is finished the birds congregate in large numbers. From one garden it was possible to see between 1200 and 1500 in flight, an indication that the Parrakeet population in Delhi is immense.

DOUGLAS DEWAR

Douglas Dewar ("The Common Birds of India," published in India) was writing many years before Whistler or Smythies. Yet his observations are also still very relevant today (**opposite**) :

THE GREEN PARROTS

As all the green parrots have the same habits, it will suffice to describe those of one species. Let us then consider those of the widely-distributed group of large Indian Parrakeets.

The large Indian Parrakeet (Palaeornis nepalensis) is found throughout Northern and Central India. It extends as far south as Kandesh. Its eastern limits cannot be fixed with precision, because in Sikkim, Assam and the Sunderbuns it runs into the Burmese species, with which it interbreeds freely, producing crosses which are intermediate in appearance between the two species.

The large Indian Parrakeet which Jerdon styled the **Alexandrine** Parrakeet, is, like all the Indian green parrots, a very handsome bird. In length it measures 21 inches, of which the flowing tail accounts for a trifle over 12. The prevailing hue of the plumage is rich green, that of grass in England after an April shower. This green is washed faintly with grey on the head, blue on the middle of the tail, and yellow at the tip of that appendage. There is a large deep-red patch, considerably longer than it is broad, on each wing. This peculiar wing-patch is a feature of several of the parrakeets. The male has a beautiful rose-pink collar round the back of the neck (or rather the head), which is met at each extremity by a broad black band that runs to the base of the beak. The bill is deep red and the eye yellow.

The **Ceylon variety**, which is 19 inches long, is known as the large Ceylonese Parrakeet (P. eupatria). The black bands running from the pink collar to the base of the bill, technically called mandibular bands, are narrower.

The **Burmese race** – the large Burmese Parrakeet (P. indoburmanicus*) which is 22 inches long, has, like the Ceylon race, narrow mandibular bands. The green in the plumage is brighter and the throat is tinged with yellow.

The **Andaman race** – the large Andaman Parrakeet (P. magnirostris) is 23 inches long. As the scientific name denotes, the bill is very large. The wing patch is of brighter red, and there is a narrow blue collar above the pink one. Traces of such a blue collar occur in some Burmese birds.

These slight differences in the four races of large green Parrakeets are due to the fact that the birds do not migrate, so that the individuals which live in one part of the country have no opportunity of mating with those of distant parts; in consequence local peculiarities, such as the blue upper collar, are not swamped by their possessors breeding with individuals which have no such collar and live at a distance.

The large Indian Parrakeet feeds on grain and fruit, and, in places where it is numerous, does much harm to the crops. A flock of hundred or more, each member of which will break off half a dozen or more heads of corn in a day, destroys a considerable percentage of the produce of the fields that the flock visits. It is to stop, as far as possible, the depredations of parrots, deer and tne many other grain-eating creatures that the Indian cultivator finds it nec-

*The name has now changed : see Chapter on descriptions

essary to erect a machan (shelter) in the middle of his field.   In this he spends the greater part of the day and night from the time that the grain begins to form until it is harvested.

The Indian native gets something of his own back by capturing large numbers of young parrots and selling them for a few annas as a cage bird. Verily are the sins of the parents visited on the children, for most of these caged parrots are taken out of the nest before they have begun to levy toll on the ripening crops. These unfortunate birds are kept in tiny iron cages in which they are so cramped that they would die but for the fact that they are able to get sufficient exercise to keep them in fair health by climbing about the inside of their prison, beak over claw, and by standing on the solitary perch bending back the neck and wagging the head from side to side in such a way that one cannot understand why they do not fall off the perch from giddiness. Those who keep parrots are fond of them and are not intentionally cruel, but they often forget that the little metal cages in which parrots are confined become veritable infernos when hung out in the sun.

Indian Parrakeets can sometimes be taught to talk and to imitate sounds, but as a rule they are not good talkers or mimics.

Thanks to the large number that are taken captive, green parrots are not such serious pests as they would be were not their numbers kept down in this way, but they are still a scourge in many parts of the country and the agricultural departments of the various Governments might with advantage consider the advisability of taking steps to thin out some species. As their feathers form a pretty decoration for a woman's hat, some parrots might be shot and sold for this purpose to milliners in countries where bird protection is not carried to extremes, as it is in England where the Government is in the habit of yielding to the clamour of faddists!

The flight of green parrots is swift and as straight as the proverbial die. As they dash overhead in noisy flocks they look like living emeralds. Green parrots nest in holes, usually in trees, occasionally in buildings. If they can find a suitable ready-made cavity they utilise this, otherwise they scoop out a nest-hole by means of the powerful bill. Sometimes squabbles over nest-holes arise between parrots and mynas. In such cases the Mynas usually triumph, owing to their pertinacity, which is often more than a match for Polly's superior bill-power.

Courting Parrakeets go through the most absurd performances, in which head-tickling plays a prominent part. From two to four white eggs are laid. Green parrots lay their eggs in any of the first six months of the year. In Northern India most eggs are laid in February.

MODERN ORNITHOLOGISTS' VIEWS

There have been many studies made of Ring Neck Parrakeets, particularly those found in Asia. Earlier writers tended to distinguish the Alexandrine and Indian Ring Necks. Thus Hugh Whistler ("Popular Handbook of Indian Birds," 1941) refers to them as:

1.   The Large Indian Parrakeet
     Psittacula eupatria (Linnaeus)
2.   The Green Parrakeet
     <u>*Psittacula kramera*</u> (Scopoli)

He notes the large Parrakeet (Alexandrine) is found in any type of terrain in which large trees are numerous. A family bird, it is found in large flocks scouring the countryside for seeds, fruits and grain which it devours in large quantities. The smaller bird has similar habits.

B.A. Smythies (*Birds of Burma*, Nimrod Press) covers the natural history as related to Burma. He calls the smaller bird the Rose–Ringed Parrakeet. He also mentions the Blossom–Headed Parrakeet and the Grey–Headed Parrakeet and appropriate sections are reproduced with due acknowledgemen to the author, who spent a considerable period in Burma working in the forests as an administrator.

The species found in Burma live in pairs in the breeding season, and at other times gather into flocks, which from their universality, the damage they do in gardens and fields, their noisiness, and their vivid coloration, are known to all and sundry. They are wonderful climbers, equally at home in any position and using their beaks freely to hold on with, and are normally arboreal in habits; but a field of ripening paddy or maize will attract them in large numbers, to the despair of the unfortunate cultivator; it is not so much the grain they eat as their very wasteful method of feeding that does the damage, for they often break of f a whole ear, select one or two grains, and throw down the rest. They are also very destructive to maize, tearing open the pods and eating unripe seeds.

On the ground their short legs, adapted for climbing or grasping food, and their long tails result in an awkward sidling gait that looks very quaint; but on the wing they are magnificent, hurtling through the forest in a compact flock and swerving gracefully to avoid trees and branches. In the open the flight is direct and is best seen in the evening when cock after cock hurry in succession along the same line to a patch of trees, where they roost together, sometimes along with crows and Mynas. Some species are commonly kept as cage birds, especially the Rose–ringed Parrakeet, but though individuals may be taught to say a few words the best of them never learn to talk as glibly as the African parrots; nevertheless there is something sedate and knowing about their demeanour that makes them attractive pets.

Most birds breed in the hot weather. No nest is made, the eggs being laid in holes in trees, or less commonly in walls or buildings. The hole may be a natural one, but the bird often excavates a tunnel and chamber similar to that of a wood–pecker. The eggs are pure white in colour.

Local names applicable to all parrakeets are -- Burmese: kyet-tu-ywe; Chingpaw: kaikke.

ALEXANDRINE PARRAKEET, *Psittacula eupatria* (Linnaeus)
SUB SPECIES: avensis (Kloss), siamensis (Kloss)
LOCAL NAMES: Burmese: Kyet-taw or kyet-paung-ka.
IDENTIFICATION.. 2O". Females and young birds lack the rose collar and the black moustachial streak.
VOICE.The cry is described as harsh and sonorous, or loud and shrill.
HABITS AND FOOD.Those of the family. It is chiefly a bird of the plains and of *indaing* forest..
NEST AND EGGS. Have been taken in Tennasserim (December), Southern Burma (February and March), and Central Burma (December to February).
STATUS AND DISTRIBUTION.   Widespread in the Oriental Region (excluding Malaysia). Sparingly distributed throughout Burma, but not north of Myitkyina or south of Amherst and not in the higher hills.

ROSE-RINGED PARRAKEET, *Psittacula krameri* (Scopoli)
SUBSPECIES; *borealis* (Neumann)
LOCAL NAME; Burmese: kyegyok

IDENTIFICATION. 16.5". Young males do not acquire the rose collar and black band until their third year, and the female has them replaced by an indistinct emerald-green band.
VOICE. The ordinary call is a harsh, rather shrill scream.
HABITS AND FOOD. Those of the family. In Burma it is a fairly common bird of the plains and uplands of the dry zone, but nowhere attains the vast numbers that are to been seen in India, where it is the commonest and most familiar of Parrakeets.
NEST AND EGGS. Not described from Burma.
STATUS AND DISTRIBUTION. Africa, India, and Central Burma. It is a bird of the dry zone, straggling thence down the Irrawaddy and Sittang valleys to about the latitude of Pegu, and eastwards to the Shan States and Karenni; there are no records from N Burma or Tenasserim.

BLOSSOM-HEADED PARAKEET, *Psittacula finschii* (Hume)
SUBSPECIES: *juneae* Biswas, *roseata* Biswas
LOCAL NAME. Burmese: *kye-tama*
IDENTIFICATION. 13.5". The female has the red on the head is replaced by adult bluish-grey and there is no black on the chin and throat and the red wing-spot is lacking; a yellow ring replaces the black collar. She is apt to be confused with the next species, but the tip of the tail, usually conspicuous in flight, is whitish, whereas in the next species it is bright yellow. Young birds are wholly green and have the bill a pale yellow.
VOICE. Its voice is softer and more musical than that of the other Parrakeets, and in flight it utters a sharp interrogative cry, *tooi* ?
HABITS AND FOOD. Those of the family. It frequents cultivation and the out- skirts of forests.

NEST AND EGGS.   Macdonald reports that they are common on Mt. Popa and breed during March and April, while Wickham found it breeding at 3,000 feet in the Shan States early in March.

STATUS AND DISTRIBUTION.   Indo-Chinese sub -region.   It is sparingly distributed through Central and Southern Burma, the Shan States, and Tenasserim (excluding Mergui district), but seems to be local nowadays, although Oates found them abundant in Southern Burma a century ago, and so did Davison in N Tenasscrim. In Arakan "generally scarce and locally migratory, but very common in March and April at Ruywa" (Christison).

GREY-HEADED PARAKEET,   *Psittacula finschii* (Hume)
LOCAL NAME. Burmese: *Kye-kala*
IDENTIFICATION. 14". The female has no red wing-patch and young birds are wholly green, but apparently acquire the slaty head in their first year.
VOICE. It has a comparatively soft and melodious though high-pitched call, constantly uttered on the wing and from trees, and a shrill whistle not unlike that of the Long-tailed Broadbill.
HABITS AND FOOD. Those of the family. It is more of a forest bird, and more of a hill bird, than the other Parrakeets. Large numbers have been seen eating grit in the dry bed of a sandy stream in Mandalay district. Others have been seen feeding on the leaf buds and farming fruits of wild cherries in Maymyo, and Davison noticed it feeding on *letpan* flowers and flowering climbers. It is a characteristic bird of the teak forests of the Pegu Yomas.
NEST AND EGGS.   In Central and Southern Burma it breeds from January to March..

ALEXANDRINES

The Alexandrines fit into the " Ring –Neck " description quite naturally. Indeed, they are really a larger version of the Indian Ring Necks. As shown in the Natural History chapter earlier writers referred to them as the **Larger Green Parrakeets**. Not all the Parrakeets in the *Psitticula* group are strictly "ring necks", a matter considered below.

FIELD NOTES ON OTHER SPECIES

Other   experiences collected from different sources are worth reproducing:

CEYLON ALEXANDRINE PARRAKEET

Leggs ("Birds of Ceylon" Vol. I., p. 170)   says: "Large colonies of this species take up their abode in districts where coconut cultivation borders on forests and wild jungle, which afford an abundance of fruit-bearing trees, on the berries of which the Alexandrine Parrakeet subsists. It is also found in openly-timbered country and in forests. It roosts in considerable numbers in coconut groves, often close to a village, pouring in about half an hour before sunset in small swiftly-flying parties from all directions, which, as their numbers increase towards the time for roosting, create a deafening noise in the excitement of choosing or finding their accustomed quarters. The fronds of the coconut afford them a favourite perch, on which they sleep huddled together in rows. At daybreak the vast crowd is again astir, and after much ado, flying from tree to tree with incessant screaming, small parties start off for their feeding-grounds, flying low, just above the trees, and every now and then uttering their full and loud note **ke-aar**; this sound is more long-drawn and not so shrill as that of the smaller bird, and can be heard at a great distance. Isolated birds have a habit of apparently leaving the rest of the flock and roaming off at a great height in the air, every now and then giving out a loud scream, which often attracts the attention of the traveller or sportsman for some little time before he is aware of the position of the Parrakeet, which is flying swiftly on far above his head. It is a shyer bird than its smaller congener, and rather difficult to approach. When not engaged in feeding or in the business of settling down for the night; at the latter time numbers may be shot without their companions doing more than flying out of, and directly returning to, their chosen trees. In the forests of the south-eastern part of the island I observed these Parrakeets resorting at evening to dead and sparsely-foliaged trees, the bare branches of which afford them a similar perch to that of the palm frond.

"They feed on grain as well as on the fruits and berries of forest trees; and I on one occasion captured a fine specimen which had become entangled in a species of vetch which covered the earthy portions of a rocky islet near Pigeon Island; it had been feeding on the seeds of the plant, and while extracting them from the pod had got beneath the tangled mass and was unable to extricate itself again. In confinement this species is possessed of the usual docility peculiar to the Parrot order, and is a very favourite pet in Ceylon with both Europeans and natives; I do not think it is as often taught to imitate the human voice as the next species, but I have heard it occasionally speak native words with a fair amount of distinctness.

Indian writers say that it is taught with facility to speak; but I think that as a general rule in Ceylon it is kept more as an ornament than for its powers of talking, and, when newly feathered, with its tail in perfect order, is a very handsome bird.

Layard writes that he was informed by natives that this bird laid two eggs, building, of course, as all Parrakeets, in a hollow tree. It excavates the hole in which it breeds, generally choosing a small limb, of which the hard shell to be cut through before reaching; the interior cavity is not very thick.

NEPALESE ALEXANDRINE PARRAKEET

Of this species Captain Hutton remarked: "Towards the end of January and beginning of February it begins to cut a circular hole in some tree wherein to lay its eggs, which are usually two in number and pure white. The tree generally in request for this purpose is the semul or cotton-tree hepta, although, sometimes, even the hard-wooded sal is chosen; the entrance-hole is a neatly-cut circle, either in the trunk or in some thick up-right branch. The trees selected by these birds are not situated in the depths of the forests, but are detached on the outskirts, and, what is curious in such a quarrelsome bird, there are often three or four nests in the same tree. The eggs are hatched in about twenty-one days, and in the middle of March the young birds are about half-fledged and are then removed for sale.

According to Willughby, writing in 1678:   "This was the first of all the Parrots brought out of India into Europe, and the only one known to the ancients for a long time, to wit, from the time of Alexander the Great to the age of Nero, by whose searchers (as Pliny witnesseth) Parrots were discovered elsewhere, viz., in Gagandi, an Island of Ethiopia.

This is perhaps the most frequently imported and best known of all the Alexandrine Parrakeets.

AFRICAN RING NECK

In its wild state this species lives chiefly in small companies in wooded steppes and on the banks of rivers where there are tall trees. It flies restlessly with much noise from tree to tree, and is very conspicuous wherever it is restless and very voracious. It devours figs, dates, tamarinds, and other fruits. Its flight is high, rapid, and direct, its long tail held quite horizontally, and the well-known whistle of the old males is abundantly heard, both when leaving and approaching the trees. The breeding season is from March to June; the careless nests are formed in hollow trees (such as acacias) at a height of from fifteen to thirty feet from the ground, and produce from three to four half-naked young, which are an unusual time in developing.

Capt. Boyd Alexander, writing on the *Birds of the Gold Coast* says:

"We observed it near Busu in December in very large flocks, frequenting the guinea-corn plantations , the corn being then nearly ripe".

The soft parts are thus described from specimens obtained on the White Nile by R. McD. Hawker: "Iris pale straw-colour; bill red, blackish at tip and on lower mandible; legs and feet grey."

My friend, Mr. James Housden, of Sydenham, had a pair of this species committed to his care by Major, then Lieut. Horsbrugh, and consequently I had an opportunity of examining them. They appeared to be slightly smaller than the Indian bird and somewhat less noisy; the size and colouring of the beak would alone serve to distinguish them at a glance from *P. k mallensis* and it is to me surprising ; that the two should have been confused. I should describe the upper mandible as crimson, blackish at tip, and more or less suffused with blackish to about the middle (as if the beak had been dipped into an ink-pot so as to dull the crimson on the distal half), the lower mandible also suffused with blackish, but to the base. In fact, the beak is altogether dingier than that of the Indian species. This species first reached the London Zoological Gardens in 1861.

Fig. 4.1 Derbyan Parrakeets

CONCLUSION

The Ring Necks survive in great numbers in their native lands. They are part of the natural habitat of these far-off lands where the climate tends to be very hot and often dry. What is remarkable is how they have adapted to domestic life in aviaries in climates so unlike their own.

Fig. 4.2 Malabar Parrakeet

5

RING NECKS IN AVICULTURE

SPECIES AVAILABLE

There are two sub-species of **Psittacula krameri:**

1. Psittacula   k.   manillensis
2. Psittacula   k.   krameri

INDIAN RING NECK *(P .k. Manillensis)*

This is the most popular of the Ring-Necked Parrakeets, being widely kept by aviculturists all over the world.

In its native India they are regarded as a pest doing damage to crops and trees. They raid orchards and fields of grain and steps have to be takento frighten them away or eliminate them.

Since the species is so common surprise may be expressed that aviculturists find it so attractive and spend considerable sums on aviaries and captive breeding programmes. The fact remains that despite its plentiful supply in India the Ring-Necked Parrakeets give great enjoyment to thous- ands who attempt to breed them each year and the production of different colours (mutations) provides a challenging and fascinating hobby.

DESCRIPTION

Adult Male

The male is distinguished at once from the female by having a ring round its neck; this ring is in two colours – one black, the other reddish. The black starts from the chinand runs nearly to the middleof the neck, but the two extremities do not quite meet in the centre; and the reddish ring starts from the sides of the face, is thickest on the back of the neck, and its extremities also fail to quite meet under the chin. The black line is above the red one. The general colour of the plumage is green, shaded with blue on the top of the head, and with yellow on the sides, the under– tail coverts, and the under surface of the tail ; the latter is blue above, and the flights have a brownish shade.

Note: The male reaches maturity and grows his ring–neck at 2–3 years
*This is the old name for the Ring-Necked Parrakeet

of age. He does not usually breed until this stage is reached. However, he may attempt to breed earlier but the eggs may be infertile.

Adult Female

Similar to the male, but no ring on the neck. It is predominantly a bright, apple green. Some descriptions suggst shorter central tail feathers but often females have very long tails and judging on this feature alone could be misleading.

SIZE

The length is 40 cm (l6in.) and about l2.5cm (5 in.) is the tail.

ALTERNATIVE DESCRIPTION

A supplementary description, giving more detail, is given by Dr. J.M. Bechstein (*Cage and Chamber Birds*) and is in such simple terms that reproduction is worthwhile:

The Rose-Ringed Parrakeet *

Psittacus Manillensis, BECH. Varietas : *Psittaci Alexandri,* Lin. Perruche a collier couleur de rose, BUF. Der rosennachige Sittich, BECH.

Description – This very beautiful Parrot, remarkable for the softness of its colours and the silkiness of its plumage, is about the size of a Missel Thrush. Its total length, including the tail, which makes up at least two thirds, is fourteen or fifteen inches. The two centre tail feathers are three inches and a half longer than the exterior ones. The beak is three quarters of an inch long, strong, very much curved, and crimson on the upper side; below blackish blue. The membrane of the beak is flesh-coloured; the eye-lids bright red; the iris white, with a blueish tinge; the feet greyish brown. The plumage is generally light green; darker on the upper part of the body, and in the lower almost yellow. From the black throat a band, which is first black and then pale rose colour, extends round the head; and in old birds the nape of the neck has a blue tinge. There is a darker shade on the wing coverts and the scapulars, and the edges of the pen feathers are also darker. The rump, the tail coverts, as well as the first four side feathers of the tail itself, are greenish yellow; the two centre feathers, however, from the middle to the tip, which is green, are a greenish blue. The black on the throat of the female is not so extensive, nor has it the rose-coloured neck band. The under part of the body also is more inclined to yellow.

AFRICAN RING-NECK (*P.k krameri*)

Usually a little smaller than the Indian Ring Neck and not as popular in aviculture it is, nevertheless, kept and successful breeding has occurred. The tail is smooth and the beak is a darker colour – usually described as a "blackish-red" or "dusky-red". Some, writers have indicated that such a minor difference may be a difficult indication to allow a distinction to be made between the two species. The beak is darker and sometimes

Fig 5.1 Group of Parrakeets

Blossom Headed Parrakeet   Ring-Necked Parrakeet
            Quaker Parrakeet
        (Not Ring Neck)

ALEXANDRINE – DETAILED DESCRIPTION

Dr. A. G. Butler described the Alexandrine in the following terms:

Cinghalese Alexandrine Parrakeet
(Psitticula eupatria)

Above grass-green; wings darker green; a dark red patch on the secondary wing-coverts; central tail feathers   green at base, then changing to blue, and yellowish at tips; forehead and   lores brighter green; a blackish stripe from nostrils to eye; back of head and cheeks tinged with greyish blue; a broad black stripe from beak downwards and across sides of neck,   where it meets a rose-coloured collar round back of neck;   under surface dingy green,   excepting on abdomen and under tail-coverts, which are brighter; greater under wing-coverts and flights below slate-grey; tail below yellowish; beak deep cherry red, paler on lower mandible, yellowish at tip; feet sap-green or leaden-grey irides pale yellow, with greyish inner circle; eyelid dull reddish. Female rather smaller; without black stripe from beak round neck, and rose collar.

Nepalese Alexandrine Parrakeet
(Psitticula nepalensis)

Much larger than the preceding species, but otherwise (excepting that the back of head and cheeks are greyer) similar in both sexes.

Hab., North and Central India.

Jerdon confounds this with the other forms of Alexandrine Parrakeets, so that his notes on the habits need not be quoted here. Hume also unites them all under one heading, but notes the habitat under each observation. He says: "The Rose-band Paroquet breeds in the Kangra Valley in April, laying four eggs in large holes in trees, excavated by the birds themselves. Though I have found plenty of nests with young, I have never taken the egg myself........."

Great-Billed Alexandrine Parrakeet
(Psitticula magnirostris)

Differs from the preceding in its much larger and stronger beak; beak bright red, the tip yellow; cere yellow; feet orange-yellow; irides bright yellow; eye-lids pale pink, with orange edges. Female smaller; without the black stripe and rose-red collar.

Hab., Andaman Islands.

Indo-Burmese Alexandrine Parrakeets

Differs from the preceding in the brighter red patch on the wing-coverts and in having a narrow blue collar above the rose-coloured one on the back of the neck; beak bright red with yellow tip. Female smaller and without the black stripe and collar.

Hab., Sikkim to Tenasserim and eastwards to Cambodia.

OTHER RELATED SPECIES

As noted earlier Ring Necked Parrakeets belong to tne genus PSITTAC–ULA. This includes many species all of which have long tails, with the central pair being longest of all. Which should be classified as ring–necks is difficult to determine because strictly the Psittacula krameri krameri and its sub–species are the ring–necks. On the other hand, the Alexandrines are undoubtedly Ring–necked despite the different name.

The Plum–Headed and Blossom Headed also exhibit distinct rings, usually in the form of a moustache.

A complete list of Psittacula is as follows:

1. Alexandrine (5 sub–species)
2. Blossom–Headed (2)
3. Blyth's
4. Derbyan (Lord Derby's)
5. Emerald Collared (Layard's)
6. Long–Tailed (5)
7. Malabar
8. Mauritius
9. Moustached (8)
10. Newton's
11 Plum–Headed
12. Ring–Necked (4)
13. Red–Cheeked
14. Rose–Headed
15. Slaty–Headed (2)

A Seychelles Parrakeet also existed but is now extinct. With the remaining species (12) above, the Ring–Necked remain the most popular and (1) the Alexandrines are probably next in line.

Other species vary in popularity and availability.   In warmer climates such as in the U.S.A. and Australia more success has been achieved with the less popular varieties.

Recent advertisements in magazines in the U.K. indicated availability of the following on a fairly common basis:

(a) Ring–Necks Indian and African
(b) Plum–Headed
(c) Alexandrines

Others available were (15) Slaty–Headed and (4) Derbyan. In Ring Necks mutations readily available were Lutinos, Blues, Greys and Albinos in that order.

DESCRIPTIONS OF SOME OF LESS COMMON SPECIES

Blossom-Headed Parrakeet

The cock bird, when adult, is of a brilliant green colour, the head having a beautiful peach-like colouring, red, shaded with blue, at the back and the nape of the neck, and less distinctly on the cheeks. There is a black stripe from the lower mandible, which is continued as a collar round tne neck, and is followed by a yellowish ring. The lesser wing-coverts are marked with a bright cinnamon reddish patch; the axillaries and under wing-coverts are of a glaucous or verditer blue colour. The two central tail-feathers are blue, tipped with white, an the remainder green, tipped with yellow. The upper mandible is waxy yellow, varying to orange, and the lower mandible black or dusky. The hen has no back collar or red patch on the wing-coverts; the top, back, and sides of the head are lilacine, somewhat browner on the sides, and bounded by a better defined yellow collar. The black collar is wanting.

Hab., Himalayas, the northern, western, and southern portion of Central India, and Ceylon.

Derbyan Parrakeet

Green; more yellow on centre of wings; lateral tail-feather above with a slight bluish tinge on outer webs; four central feathers blue, broadly edged with green towards the base; forehead, lores and a broad moustachial streak velvety-black; front of crown and orbital region verditer green; back of crown and ear-coverts violoceous blue; a narrow vinous line from back of ear-coverts down the side of the neck; the underwing-coverts and under surface to vent similarly coloured; undertail-coverts green narrowly edged with blueish; tail below dull golden-olive; beak black; irides pale straw-colour. Female with the upper mandible red.

Hab., "interior of China," probably Hainan.

Malabar Parrakeet

Green, somewhat bluer above than below; the head, neck, upper back, and breast ashy-grey, with the exception of the forehead, which is green edged behind with blue; the lores and a patch encircling the eyes, which are green; From the beak runs a broad black moustachial stripe which joins a black collar bordered behind by blueish colour which becomes broader on the throat; upper wing-coverts with pale edges; first primary black, the others blue edged with green; central tail feathers blue, greenish at the base, and tipped with yellowish; next pair blue on the outer web, greenish towards the base; remaining feathers with blue outer and yellow inner webs; all the tips and the under surface yellow; upper mandible red with worn-white point, lower mandible dusky reddish; feet greenish leaden; iris varying from yellow brown.

Slaty-Headed Parrakeet

Green; hind-neck tinged with verdigris; a dark cherry-red patch on median wing-coverts; front edge of wing yellow; primaries with dark green outer webs with narrow yellowish edge, dark grey inner webs; central tail-feathers more or less green at base, blue in the middle, bright yellow on distal half, the other feathers green on outer and yellow on inner webs; head slaty blueish-black; chin, mandibular stripe and a narrow collar at the back of neck, black; under parts paler and more yellowish-green than above; under wing-coverts verdigris; tail below yellow; beak with coral-red upper mandible, the terminal hook and lower mandible yellow; feet dusky green; iris straw-colour; orbital skin slaty. Female without the dark red wing-patch.

Hab., North India where, according to Hume, "it is confined to a narrow zone lying between the bases of the sub-Himalayan ranges and the first high snowy ridge."

For descriptions of other species the reader is referred to : *Parrots of the World*, Forshaw and Cooper (see Bibliography).

6

ACCOMMODATION

POSSIBLE APPROACHES

Birds in captivity may be kept in a variety of ways:

1. Cages

2. Small Flights

3. Aviaries (including an adjoining Bird-room)

Modern fanciers now recognise that cages and stands are too restrictive for all Parrot-like birds. There has been an upsurge in animal welfare interest and, whether this is always genuine or not, the fact remains that people are made aware that restrictions in themselves must be harmful to the occupants. Obviously even an aviary can be harmful if not designed correctly or much too small.

Inadequate flying space is unnatural for a bird made to fly from one tree to another. Moreover, the lack of exercise must give rise to health problems fatty tissue will develop – and it is unlikely that birds will breed. However, it must also be stressed that some species may not breed if given too much space. The author has experimented with pigeons and small parrots with different sizes of accommodation. It was found that when placed in quite large open aviaries the birds failed to breed – yet in a small covered aviary they had bred on a regular basis. A size compatible with the species should be the aim.

DISADVANTAGES OF CAGES AND SMALL ENCLOSURES

Psychological studies have been made of birds kept in small units such as cages. The effects are summarized below:

1. Boredom

Parrakeets which are bored may resort to feather pecking and other bad habits which makes them quite unsightly. Human contact and giving a wide

Parrakeets which are bored may resort to feather pecking and other bad habits which makes them quite unsightly. Human contact and giving a wide variety of food may offset this tendency, but only partially.

2. Loss of Escape Routes

No matter how tame birds become they will react by flying or screeching. The author's Ring–Necks fly from one side of the aviary to the other, climb the wire netting, gripping it with their beaks and generally acting in a normal manner. Once they settle down there is no problem but this natural reaction cannot be avoided. In a cage the bird cannot escape and is a prisoner in every sense; there is no escape route so passive acceptance results and there is an inevitable loss of natural behaviour.

3. Lack of Exercise

Birds love to fly from perch to perch. They also relish food – seeds of various sorts – thrown on to the floor of the aviary where it starts to sprout. This is the normal behaviour pattern– Parrakeets alight on forest floors and pick up food. This searching for food is beneficial to the bird and in some cases it be found that the ground–feeding species will limit the food intake.

4. Impact on Breeding

In a very restricted space Parrakeets will not breed. Even in an aviary the number of failures is quite high. Putting a male and female together and hoping they will be compatible is fraught with difficulties. Some experts believe this incompatibility to be the cause of most failures.

These are the most obvious; other problems are considered in the chapter which deals with breeding.

AVIARIES FOR RING NECKS

Ring Necks may be kept in aviaries throughout the year. if bred in captivity they are hardy and quite happy in "limited" accommodation. Although they may be kept in cages this is not to be recommended. They are active, boisterous birds, constantly flying, so too much restriction is cruel and will lead to frustration and bad habits.

Aviaries Should be for Specific Purpose

A small aviary 6 ft. x 4 ft. will be quite adequate for keeping a pair of Ring Necks. Indeed, 4 or 5 birds may be kept in this size area and live quite happily. **Careful siting of perches and the provision of shelves on which trays are kept will help to make the most of the aviary**

The addition of a **verandah,** let into the side of the aviary, also gives

When birds are to breed a larger aviary may be necessary. Obviously the larger the aviary which can be given the better it will be for the captive birds. Sizes like 24 ft. long x 8 ft. wide and 10 ft high are recommended, but these are outside the capabilities of most /amateur bird-keepers. Indeed, if one pair per aviary is to be the rule the proposition becomes impossible.

Recent experiences of breeders suggest the following:

1. A large Communal Aviary

Whether this will succeed or not depends on a variety of factors. Generally speaking Parrakeets should be housed separately (in pairs) for breeding. However, in a very large aviary, with numerous nesting places and boxes, with adequate cover for birds to be private Ring Necks may breed in a communal aviary. Generally the private fancier (as opposed to a Zoo) has small aviaries.

2. Blocks

Aviaries side –by– side in blocks. Provided the birds can fly a considerable distance the fact that an aviary is narrow does not seem to matter. However, to be practical a minimum width of 1 metre is advisable.

3. Single Aviaries and Sleeping Compartments

This is likely to be the type used by many fanciers. A small area – possibly half of a bird room – can be used for sleeping and the balance is for flying. A garden shed (8 ft x 4 ft) can be divided by a partition and an entrance hole provided at each side which leads into an aviary. In practice many other variations may be found.

SPECIAL REQUIREMENTS FOR AVIARY

At the outset it should be recognised that Ring Necks are strong, active birds ever gnawing at wood in the aviary, particularly as it ages and becomes dry or the least bit rotten.

The birds are provided with a very strong beak for chewing wood so obviously expect destruction to occur – it is an inevitable and natural process. Boards left exposed,without wire netting protection, will be quickly chewed tnrough.Many a bird keeper has gone to see his birds and discovered large chunks of the interior of the roof torn away and the birds still in captivity only because of thc roofing felt. Ring Necks will not usually chew any material which is covered in tar or not understood,but do not count on this tendency.

Recommendations (used by bird-keepers) are:

(a) Put wire netting or twilweld inside the aviary; i.e. have the wooden posts outside.

Safety
Porch

Perspex
Roofed
Covered
Area

Entrance
Hatch

Grass

3' 0"   3' 0"   21' 0"

Perspex panels in shelter roof   Raised levels

Partition   Rocks and logs used as Aviary "Furniture"

Raised block containing heating coil   Perimeter planting

Strong springs on all outside doors

Anti-predator overhang

Partition

Varying ground levels
Drain through the wall

Deep foundations

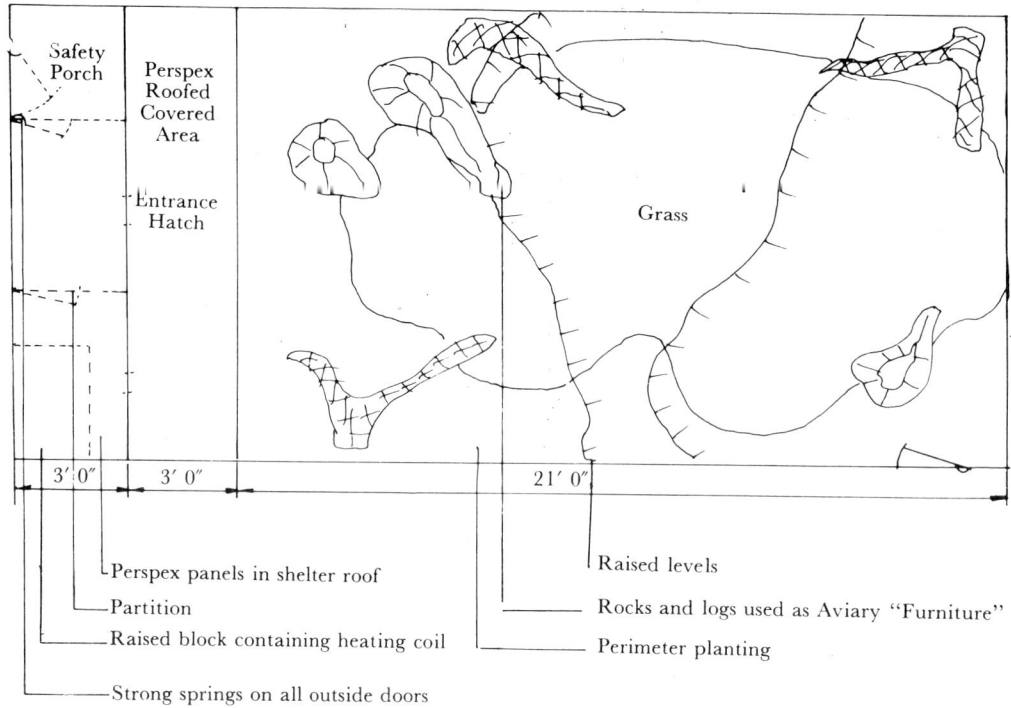

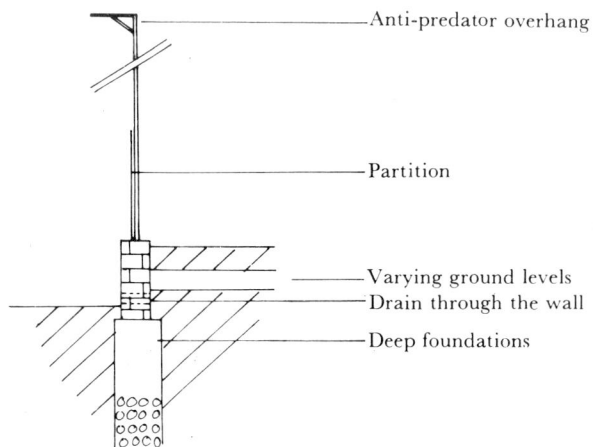

Fig. 6.1 Aviary designed by D. Grenville Roles for Pheasants (can be adapted for Parrakeets-- the importance of landscaping is emphasised)

(b) Cover wooden posts with wire netting.

(c) Give the birds plenty of wood to chew; e.g. stout branches from apple trees.

(d) Use steel posts for the main framework of the aviary. This method has been used with great success in Bird and Zoological Gardens, but it does not always look as good as natural wood.

PERCHES

A plentiful supply of wooden perches should be provided of various thicknesses. Remember, the birds like variety for walking on, flying across the aviary and for gripping when resting.

The ideal thickness for flying onto and gripping is around 0.75 to 1.00 inch (25 to 30 mm). Ring Necks are able to grip that size quite comfortably. The back toes can grip without fear of slipping.

For walks and for chewing old stakes made of beech seem ideal. With the outer bark left on they provide an ideal area where the bird walks – at times struts or swaggers *– from one side to the other.A diameter of four or five inches (say l0 cm) appears ideal. A long pole going across not only provides the footpath, but also allows a network of smaller perches to go across, being supported at one end on the thick stake or branch.

The choice of wood is not vital, but woods such as Yew should be avoided. I have found that Rhodedendron branches are ideal for perches, whereas apple branches give a good supply of chewing material. Very often it is a question of availability. If only straight pieces are available from a saw mill or wood yard then skim the sharp edges from the tops (rounding them) so that they are better to grip. The birds will soon smooth them down with wear and tear.

Whether to use round or square perches is a question which arises. Generally speaking for all birds a rounded perch is advisable. It is more natural and comfortable, allowing the Parrakeet to grip without difficulty. When a bird flies across an aviary he expects to be able to land safely and good strong perches are vital.

With Ring-Necks the experience of the author has been that square perches very quickly become rounded anyway, simply by the action of gnawing that takes place. Alexandrines in particular are quite destructive and within a few weeks will take off all the square edges.

Positioning Perches

Care should be taken to position the perches in the most convenient places attempting the following:

(a) Maximise flying space.

*The walk is unusual —— a sort of sidling gait.

(b) Try to discourage birds from flying from one side of the aviary to the other, **using the wire netting for landing**. A much better plan is to place a perch across the aviary in front of the wire so that the birds land on the perch. It is mucn more natural and better for the birds especially on a cold day with frost on the wire.

(c) Discourage them from "perching" on a night by holding on to the wire netting. Their toes may be damaged by frost or predators – who are not averse to biting off toes.

(d) Pay attention to the positioning of the door and the placing of the perches. If there is no safety porch the door should be placed away from where the birds fly when exercising from one side to the other. After a while the birds become accustomed to the keeper entering the door, but obviously there should be a watchfulness to make sure a bird does not attempt to escape. Remember that if a Parrakeet feels trapped or he is being caught then he will try to escape; this is why there must be plenty of flying space away from the door.

Wire Mesh

Parrots and Parrot-like birds require fairly strong netting which may be:

1. Conventional wire-netting

2. Weld mesh which has perfect]y joined squares or rectangles giving a neat appearance.

There is a tendency to use weld mesh these days although in fact wire netting is quite adequate and may be cheaper. The thickness should be appropriate for the birds being kept, thus:

Parrakeets

.5 x .5 inch (12mm) 16 wire guage thick

Parrots

1 inch x 1 inch (25mm) and 12 guage thick.

Remember it is also desirable to keep wild birds out of the aviary so a small size is preferable, but note the cost rises dramatically when the smaller sizes are used.

ACCOMMODATION

Essentials for an aviary are as follows:

1. Solid timber preferably lined with some form of insulating board (not soft material which the birds can peck away). Tongue and grooved boarding is very desirable because this avoids draughts. Usually .75 inch board (around 30mm) is recommended.

2. The roof should be watertight and easily maintained (a coat of tar and creosote each year should keep it in good order). Perspex sheets give adequate light, but tend to be cold in winter and hot in summer, although they are acceptable for the covered flight which has wire netting on the outside. Boards and roofing felt are probably the best method for keeping the shed dry, but remember that adequate lighting is still essential within the shed.

3. Windows and entrance holes should be provided for adequate light and exits (which also give some ventilation).
Windows should be made so they can be opened, but without draughts, and properly wire netted so that the birds cannot escape through openings. In addition, shutters or circular outlets fitted to the sides may be used for:

> a) ventilation;
> or
> b) allowing birds to fly through the openings into the outdoor flights (it may be desirable to close these in winter)

4. The floor should be made of wood (above the ground) or concrete. Thick timber, well supported is essential or rats, mice and other vermin will find their way in. Moreover, if not raised above the earth the wood will rot and after a few years will let in damp and cold. Concrete is obviously the answer, but this tends to be cold so a good covering of clean wood shavings is essential (renewed when it becomes soiled). Alternatively, a shed with a wooden door can be placed on concrete or flagstones.

The Bird Room

Aviary and Bird-Room tend to be descriptions of the same thing. However, some people prefer to refer to a bird-room as a specially fitted building, or a room within a building, where all essentials can be kept and the birds can be housed in considerable comfort. Certainly for successful all-the-year-round management, well-built insulated accommodation is vital.

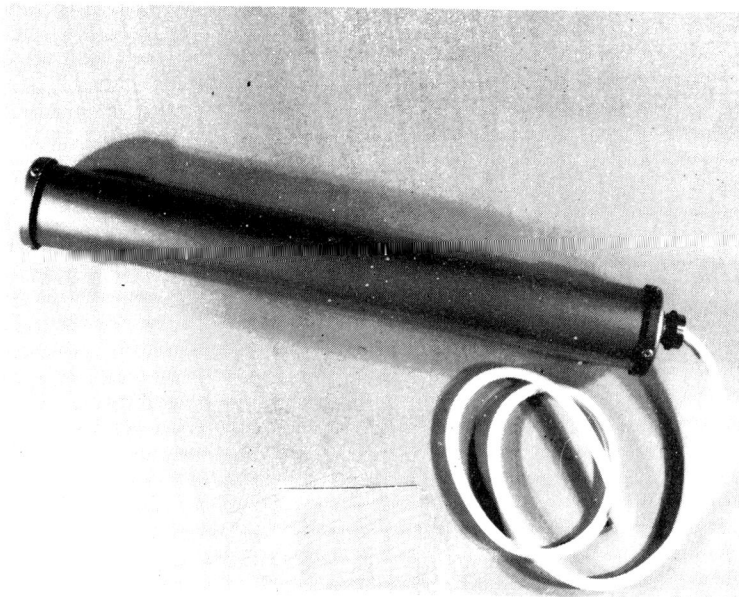

Fig . 6.2 Tubular Heater for heating in very cold weather   (Courtesy
Bartholomews of Hampshire)

Fig. 6.3 Typical Lighting Controls for Aviaries

An aviary purchased from a garden centre will probably have all the essentials for keeping a few birds, but it will not provide them with all their needs for successful breeding and showing.

If space permits an aviary and bird-room may be advisable, thus allowing birds to be kept in comfort at all times as well as providing the means for training for shows. Taken to the ultimate there should also be provision for running water indoors and electricity for light and heat.

INSULATION AND VENTILATION

The aviary or bird-room should be insulated so as to avoid extremes in temperature. If a brick building is used then a wooden frame can be built into the structure with some form of cavity and the inner skin would be plaster board, hard board or one of the many special boards now available. Polystyrene tiles are not suitable because they tend to flake and are a fire hazard. However, some manufacturers have produced special insulating materials for commercial poultry sheds and these could well be worth investigating. Remember though that unless protected with wire netting some parrots will chew all in sight.

VENTILATION

The provision of adequate air without excessive draughts should receive attention. This question is also linked with the provision of windows, which may be allowed to open with metal gauze or wire netting to cover the opening. Small holes drilled in the side of the shed will also provide ventilation as will some form of grille on arrangement which will open and close.

Ideally the inlet for air should be towards the top of the building. When the air enters it sinks to the ground and, when warmed up, will rise and may be let out at roof level. If the inlet opening is too near the bottom of the building the inrush of air will be too fierce and will cause discomfort.

The aim should be to get the air to circulate so as to remove any foul air or gases, but not to make the aviary too cold. Accordingly, the outside temperature should be considered and in the summer months wire netting covered openings could be beneficial. In winter a different story emerges because the conservation of heat is important, even if there is some loss of ventilation in the bird-room proper (ie, sleeping quarters). Except on very bad days (cold or wet) the birds should always be allowed access to a flight and thereby breathe a plentiful supply of fresh air.

Some breeders never use any heat in a bird-room, whereas others insist that no results are possible without the means of keeping the temperature at not less than around 50°F. Certainly for making an early start with breeding and to make sure that water does not freeze some form of heating is advisable.

In modern times the tendency is to employ tubular heaters which are totally enclosed and use a small amount of electricity. A typical heater is shown opposite; it is usually supplied in convenient lengths of around 1 metre upwards and can be attend easily and requires no maintenance. Because of its lower power consumption it may be operated without a thermostat, simply being turned off when the weather is mild.

The position of the aviary also affects heat and light. The author has an aviary at the side of a large lawn with hedges on one side and a wire netting front at the other. Any day when there is sun its rays catch the front of the aviary and give light and warmth. On the other hand, a shed and aviary in a wooded area tends to be extremely suitable in the Summer, but is bitterly cold in Winter. In such circumstances the author has had bantams succumb to the severe frosts which accumulate in the trees so imagine what can happen to an aviary bird.

This is not to suggest that parrot-like birds are not hardy. They will stand considerable cold and variations in weather once acclimatised, but if early breeding is required with fertile eggs from the first clutch of eggs then give them shelter from cold winds, snow and rain.

LIGHTING

Light affects birds and provides the stimulation to lay. Accordingly, the provision of adequate light is desirable in two forms:

a) Windows and netted fronts

b) Electric light controlled by a time switch so that the desired amount of light can be given.

There is no hard and fast rule on the length of period of lighting to give. On poultry breeding and laying there has been considerable research and broadly speaking around 16-17 hours light is regarded as standard at which to aim. This means the automatic switch is regulated to bring on the light early in the morning to cut off when natural light is adequate and then to switch back on for a further period in the evening.

An alternative is to turn on the light from a switch in the house and then turn it off last thing at night. If this is done a day of around 12 hours is the norm and many breeders have found this acceptable.   Cert - ainly if too much light is given there is a danger of stress to the birds. The intensity of light is also important; a small wattage will be adequate, say, 25 watts for an 8 x 6ft house.

Painting the building inside with a white paint will also affect the light. Lighter paints reflect light better than the darker shades so obviously it is better to use white or some other light colour. Outdoor emulsion or an oil-based paint is advisable.

PROTECTION FROM DISEASE AND PREDATORS

Birds should be protected from disease and provided common sense rules are allowed there should be no problem. Some of the more obvious precautions are as follows:

1. Feed good quality food and watch for mould or bacteria appearing.

2. Clean out food hoppers on a regular basis.

3. Remove sand or sawdust used on the floor at regular intervals. Make sure cobwebs are removed and go round breeding cages with a vacuum cleaner removing all dust – obviously removing birds before this is done. Give this a thorough clean at least once a year, preferably twice, and make sure every part is cleaned and disinfected. Also clean out cupboards and any place where vermin may lurk.

4. Spray the cages and stock with anti-mite spray and check that the birds are free from parasites. A check should be made at night with torch light to see if red mite exist.

5. Watch out for small access holes gnawed by mice or other creatures (including Parrot-like birds!) and block these. If the invasion persists place bait where mice can get it, but well away from the birds.

6. Keep adequate water in the house and change it regularly. Wash out the utensils in a mild solution of disinfectant (suitable for the purpose) and then rinse thoroughly with clean running water.

7. Have a bird bath so the birds can keep themselves clean.

8. Wash fresh green food stuff in a colander and then remove all surplus. A salad strainer is ideal for this purpose. With insecticides being used the washing is a precaution in case the green food has been sprayed. Where chick weed and other greens are grown in the garden it may be quite safe to feed without washing.

9. The outside flight should have a floor of small pebbles, or gravel, which can be washed down. Alternatively, grass may be sown, although this is not likely to last very long with a number of birds in captivity. Concrete floors are a possibility, but these tend to be cold and should be covered with earth or sand. They at least keep out predators. On that subject it is advisable to block the bottom of a flight so that it is predator proof. Putting wire into the ground and concreting under the bottom cross pieces is advisable or rats, cats, squirrels

and other nuisances will gain access.

10. Observe the birds carefully and when illness is apparent isolate the birds in question and ,where appropriate, use the hospital cage or a separate room which is kept quite warm.

PERCHES AND RELATED EQUIPMENT

Parrots and Parrakeets are perch users and, therefore, perches must be regarded as an essential part of the equipment of the bird-room and flight. There are a number of places to consider:
1. Cages
 Perches are placed from front to back and arranged so that the occupants can jump and fly from one to the other . Cages are not recommended for Ring Necks

2. Birdrooms
Neat uniform perches may be employed, positioned so that some are higher than others thus enabling the birds to fly around.

3. Flights or outdoor aviaries
Natural perches made from the fallen branches of pine trees or fruit trees provide an excellent means of giving all that is necessary with the added advantage of being pleasing in appearance. Branches containing twigs can be nailed into position in the corners or hanging from the ceiling and the birds enjoy moving from one section to another. Perches should be of varying sizes and may be oval or round. The earlier fanciers seemed to prefer the round type whereas today the oval-shaped are the first choice.

The fact remains that the size should be adequate for the bird to exercise its feet, at least 1 inch (25mm) ,and there are some points to watch:

a) Use soft wood rather than hard and/or slippery wood.

b) Ensure that the perch is firm so that it does not slip around when the bird alights.

c) For outside flights keep the perches away from the wire netting or cats may attack the birds whilst they are perching.

d) In siting perches in an outside flight remember to leave sufficient space for flying. Poor positioning of perches and branches may restrict the area available for flight.

SAFETY PORCHES

Access to buildings and aviaries without danger of losing birds is an essential consideration when planning accommodation. The most simple way is to have a large shed and then have a "porch" inside which allows easy access. The main compartment is kept separate with an independent door.

The disadvantage with this method is the fact that part of the bird house is wasted although this may be used to store food and equipment in regular use. Shelves can be placed on the walls and tins and boxes kept there.

Other possibilities are as follows:

1. Double Door

A solid door outside and wire netting inside will allow access (with care) but can be hazardous when going in and out. Such an arrangement can be used to keep a bird-room cool in the summer.

2. External Porch

A porch may be built on to the external door so that easy access is possible. A person entering, steps inside and then closes the door before opening the main door to the bird-room without difficulty.

Many fanciers rely on an external aviary as a form of porch, but in this case great care must be taken to ensure that birds do not fly out when the door is opened.

Landscaping

Landscaping is the designing of the aviary and the surrounding areas so that they are pleasing to the eye and more attractive to the birds. Possible additions are as follows:

1. Rustic poles for the outside flight.
2. Climbing shrubs up the side of the flight.
3. A small pond with a fountain.
4. Evergreen shrubs such as laurel and rhododendron outside the bird-room and flight.
5. Ornate structures, including brick buildings, tiled roof, elaborate windows and wrought ironwork.

The *aesthetic* requirements relate to the appearance of the aviary. Looking at a design in a negative way we can suggest that the following features should be avoided :

a)   Corrugated sheets which tend to rust and look unsightly (although properly maintained they may be acceptable for the bottom of a flight).

b)   Sheds which are knocked together from off-pieces of wood and appear untidy and look amateurish.   If the fancier is to make his own bird-houses then they must be done to an acceptable standard.

c)   Aviaries which are not maintained properly so that felt is hanging on the roof and boards are rotting for lack of paint or preservative.

Parrot-like birds will do well in garden aviaries, where, contrary to generally received opinion, they will live quite comfortably all the year round, as regardless of the weather as our common sparrows, or even more so. The birds in an aviary have no anxiety about food, or any trouble in finding or getting at it; and if they have a dry place to roost in, do not seem to feel the cold at all, but will fly around and chatter as freely in the snow as if a summer sun were shining overhead.

Nesting out-of-doors
If the aviary is turfed and has shrubs growing in it, the hens will make their nests in the nest boxes provided.

Material for Nests
Parrots and parrot-like birds use bark and chips of wood for nesting. Accordingly, wood shavings would be appropriate (discussed later).

Mice
Mice are the great trouble in an outdoor aviary, and they can be kept out of it only with difficulty. The little brutes seem capable of forcing their way through almost the smallest meshed wire that is made; or, if they are baffled in that direction, they will burrow underground, often making quite long tunnels, and will get into the enclosure where least expected. By placing tin all round the aviary, bent in the shape of the letter L, they are puzzled for a long time; and if all the horizontal part and half of the upright portion of the tin plate are underground, the mice will be baffled in their attempts to gain an entrance for a longer period still. I have, however, known them work their way in through a thick layer of cement, and even through a brick wall. Small mesh wire netting may also be used.

Birch-Brooms in lieu of Shrubs
If, instead of bushes for the birds to build in, birch- brooms are planted in pots, or in the soil, they can be protected by encircling the lower part of the handle with tin, up which the mice are unable to climb. but the pests can jump to a marvellous height, and think nothing of a flying leap of from 2.5 ft to 3ft from the wall or the wire front of the aviary into a nest.

How to get rid of Mice
Should the aviarist find that nothing will keep the vermin outside his

aviary, he will have to poison them in it; but in doing this he will have to be extremely careful that his birds do not pick up any of the poison intended for their enemies. Putting in a small cage isolates the poison from the birds.

Needless to remark, when all the mice have been killed the small cage should be at once thoroughly cleansed, or better still, burned, which will effectually prevent any accident from an incautious use of it afterwards. Should more mice, after a time, appear upon the scene, they must be served in the same way, for if,they are allowed about they will sadly interfere with the nesting birds, and small will indeed be the aviarist's success where the little pests exist in any number.

Cats

Cats are altogether intolerable nuisance to the aviarist, but can be kept out of the garden by surmounting the wall with wire-netting, 2ft 6in or 3ft high, and inclined inwards at an angle of about forty-five degrees. No cat will face that, and the birds will be left in peace.

SITE FOR AVIARY

As regards the construction of a garden aviary, it is not my intention: to say much for aviaries vary infinitely, according to the taste and purse of the designer and builder; but a few general directions will not be amiss. Always select a wall or build one, if necessary) for a background or have a strong wooden windbreaker for one wall. Lawn-aviaries open to the air all round are pretty to look at, but unsafe for birds, which are exposed in them to every blast that blows; and as.the wind from some quarters is very bitter and searching, it is as well not to subject birds to its influence. The aviary should be erected against a wall that faces either south, south-west, or even south-east; but an aspect due east, or one into which north enters, must be avoided. If no other aspect is available, the fancier had better forego the delight of an outdoor aviary, and keep his birds indoors.

SHRUBS

Unless the aviary is a very large one, and not too many birds are kept in it, there will not be much use in attempting to grow plants, or even trees, within it, for the birds will soon pick them to pieces, not so much to eat as for sheer mischief, or may be occupation. The better plan is to introduce plants in pots or small tubs, which can be removed when the plants have been disfigured, and be replaced by others.

I have found ivy, euonymus, and the different kinds of elder (the common, golden, silver, and parsley-leaved) resist their attacks better than anything else. Lilac and laburnum are both poisonous, especially the latter, and must on no account be allowed in an aviary, no matter what birds are kept.

Fig 6.5 Examples of Aviaries

Top :Aviary on wall providing adequate shelter and flying area
Bottom: Ornate Aviary with limited flying area for when not breeding

7

BREEDING

BREEDING CATEGORY

Aviary birds may be classified on the basis of how they fare in the breeding season. Some are quite difficult and, indeed, are very rarely bred in captivity; others are quite easy to reproduce and may just be left to get on with it:

A possible classification might be as possible:

Category

A   Easy to breed with no special problems; e.g. Budgerigars, Cockatiels and Kakarikis

B   Fairly straight forward but sometimes presents difficulties, especially when attempting to produce mutations; e.g. Ring-Necks such as the Lutinos, but especially Blues, Greys, and Albinos.

C   Difficult to breed often taking many years of patient endeavour to achieve success; e.g. some of the larger Parrots.

D   Very difficult to breed and sometimes no record of any breeding at all ; e.g. larger, rare Parrots.

The Ring Necks would come into Category B. However, a short cut to the breeding of mutations would be to acquire a pair of the colour in question and then breed from that pair. Alternatively, purchase a single bird, a Blue or a Yellow and then breed with a normal colour. A Split; i.e. one bred from a mutation, but exhibiting a normal colouring may be paired with a normal and various colours may be produced. This is not an easy matter and success requires great patience and skill as a bird fancier. More is given on this aspect in the section dealing with colours.

PAIRING UP

A cock and a hen should be placed together in an aviary a few months before breeding is expected. In Britain this would be around November with a view to pairing up taking place by March.

If a number of Ring Necks are kept together in a communal aviary they may pair up before full maturity and, if so, they should be kept together in the separate aviary when breeding is to commence.

When an extremely large aviary is available with a plentiful supply of nest boxes breeding may be possible from a number of pairs. Clearly though there must be a watchfulness. Any progress and any serious fighting including toe biting (which could result in amputation) must call for swift action. Any birds which show excessive aggression should be separated from the family community.

Evidence of pairing up can be seen from the behaviour of the birds. They will be seen together as a pair living in harmony, whereas those that have not found a mate will tend to be aggressive, snapping at any bird which comes within striking distance.

MATING DISPLAY

Different descriptions have been given to the mating display given to the mating display of the Ring Neck. E.J. Boosey described it as follows:

The cock's courting display is the most amazing performance, as, with blazing eyes and slightly spread wings he hops, bows and squirms round the lady of his choice, giving vent all the time to a curious and not unpleasant sort of song.

The Alexandrine cock has a similar display jumping around and spreading his wings before his hen and finally feeding her as an inducement to mate.

NEST BOXES

Different types of nest boxes will be acceptable but there is a preference for the Grandfather clock type; i.e. an upright type with a hole in the upper part for entry and exit.

Alternatively, a hollowed out log may be used, but this is inaccessible and may not be easily obtainable. Measurements recommended are 1 x 1 ft. square (300 x 300 mm) and 2 ft deep (600 mm), but some prefer larger boxes.

The entrance hole should be about 4 inches in diameter or a little smaller. A strip of wire netting or twilweld should be placed inside to facilitate entry and exit.

Many breeders have suggested that better results will be obtained by placing the nest boxes in the aviary rather than the entirely covered shelter.

Nesting Material

Opinions differ on the best nest lining but some form of natural material is advised. This may be shavings, leaves, peat, coarse sawdust or decayed wood. It should be placed to a good depth, thus helping to insulate the bottom of the nest box.

A problem with Ring Necks is their tendency to chew everything in sight so a nest box of plyboard or similar material is advised. Repairs can be carried out at the end of a nesting season.

Banjo Nest Box

Some fanciers in the past have suggested that a long tunnel should be affixed to the entrance hole of the nest box (then called a "banjo" nest box). It is believed that the Ring Neck sees the long entrance as offering more privacy than the conventional form. Certainly if it does give a better feeling of security it should be used.

POSITIONING OF NEST BOXES

Most boxes should hang in secluded positions, sheltered from the direct rays of the sun. At the same time they should be accessible for inspection, especially when chicks are in the nest box. They should be checked to ensure that feeding is taking place.

THE EGGS

In captivity Ring–Necked Parrakeets usually lay one clutch of eggs and (hopefully) raise one brood of chicks. It is suggested that twice a year is a distinct possibility in the wild, but no doubt the climate influences this matter. Certainly in Britain once a year is regarded as the norm.

The egg measures 28mm x 24mm and is white in colour. Usually around four to six eggs are laid. They may differ slightly in size from one sub–species to another.

BREEDING PROBLEMS

Failures in breeding are many and varied and new findings arise quite regularly. Sadly nothing is more frustrating than constant negative results such as:

1. Non–pairing
2. Clear eggs
3. Egg binding
4. Broken eggs
5. Unreliable mothers
    (a) Unsteady on the nest

(b) Not feeding chicks when hatched, sometimes killing them.

6. Inadequate nesting facilities

FAILURE TO PAIR-UP

The failure of birds to pair up are caused by many factors. It is important to check on:

(a) Are male and female being paired?   With some parrots surgical sexing is the only safe way. Fortunately, with Ring-Necked Parrakeets the distinguishing neck markings make sure that a male is selected. However, since this does not occur until two years of age a little later the female could well turn out to be a male.

(b) Do the birds get on with each other? Incompatibility is often present with Ring Necks, The females tend to be aggressive and may turn on the male with little or no provocation.

Sometimes one bird is afraid of the other; conversely he or she may have no interest in the mating process.

(c) Unsuitable accommodation or too many distractions.

May be too noisy or there may be other birds in the aviary. Generally speaking Parrakeets should be housed in pairs so that no conflict is possible.

Ideally the birds should "mate up" before puberty. Those birds which are quite incompatible can then be separated.

CLEAR EGGS

The clear eggs after a period of incubation, say, 7 days is a indication that copulation is not taking place in a satisfactory manner. This may be due to an immature male or he may be impotent.

Often it is a combination of factors such as unsuitable housing and food. If birds are allowed to nest too early it may be found that the male is out of condition so the eggs are clear.

With Ring Necks which nest quite early (February or March) there is always a danger of clear eggs and some breeders recommend leaving nest boxes out until March so the danger of very early chicks is avoided. It may be more sensible to have an aviary which is well sheltered so that adverse weather conditions are kept away from the birds.

EGG BINDING

An aviary which gives adequate exercise is the most probable cure to

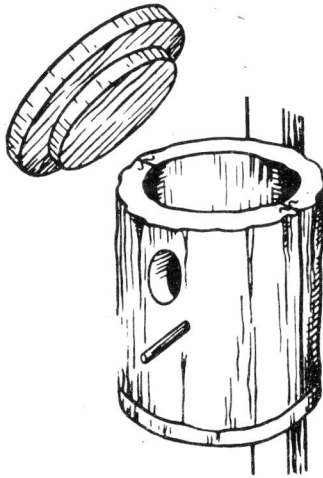

Ideal Box
although
troublesome
to make

Nest Box for
Hanging Outside
in Aviary

Hanging Bolt
(use strong cord)

Cut Hole
to Appropriate
Size

Fill with
Shavings,
Leaves
and Peat
Moss

-TREE-NEST FOR PARRAKEET.

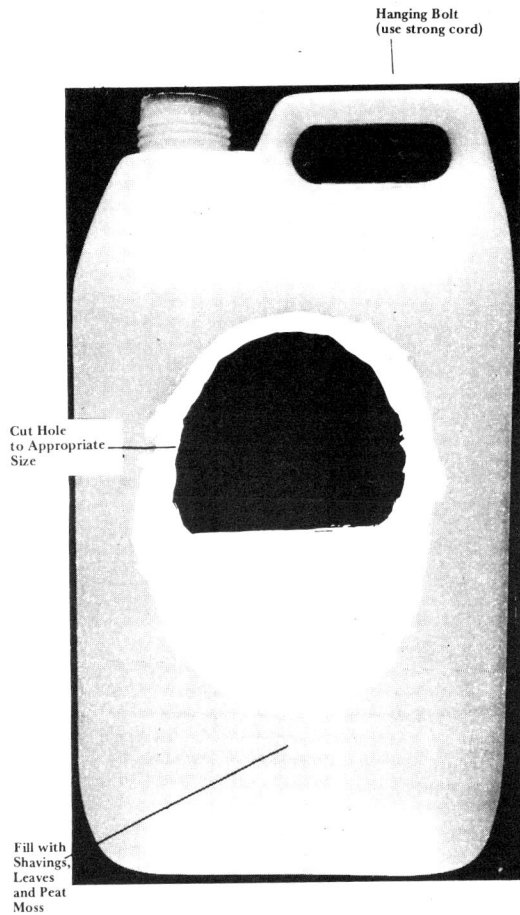

Fig.7.1 Typical Nest Boxes

Plastic Nest Box made from a discarded container.

EGG BINDING

An aviary which gives adequate exercise is the most probable cure to egg binding. If it does occur then the application of olive oil or confinement in a hospital cage may be the answer, but with good feeding practices and adequate exercise there should be no problem. Sometimes the "expression method"*, is used, but this needs great skill to press the egg out of the cloaca and can be dangerous.

BROKEN EGGS

A cock bird is often destructive and breaks the eggs. The hen may also be guilty, turning the eggs she may damage one and the harm is then done – the habit forms and many eggs are broken.

Weak shells are a common cause of the problem. Lack of grit such as cuttlefish bone or oyster shell grit may be the root of the trouble. Examine the eggs and, if they appear "patchy", with little or no lustre on the shells, they are probably suffering from lack of calcium.

The answer is to keep a plentiful supply available particularly cuttlefish bone.

UNRELIABLE MOTHER

Cannibalism and other obnoxious traits can exhibit themselves in birds without any warning. At times a young bird is involved and with maturity she will improve.

Inadequate feeding, lack of water, poor accommodation and a variety of other factors may turn the hen into an unreliable breeder. Try changing the cock and move to an alternative aviary, thus eliminating possible causes.

Constant interference with the nest box may cause desertion or other undesirable trait so try to be patient and restrict any viewing of eggs or chicks to once or twice at the most. Many hens resent any form of intrusion and become unsteady on the eggs, often being alarmed to the extent of deserting the eggs.

BREEDING RECORDS

It is at the start of the incubation and particularly the point at which the chicks are removed from their parents that records must be carefully kept, and this is especially true if the aim is to begin the establishment of a line. It will also be to the advantage of the breeder to know how the pair brought up their young, what problems were encountered, how many eggs were laid, how many were fertile or infertile, the quality of the chicks produced from any given pair in terms of size, type and feather quality and any other records which the breeder might decide are important to the continuance of the line.

*
For a detailed description see *New Zealand Parrakeets* , Batty J. Nimrod Press

Fig .7.2 African Ring-Neck Parrakeets with Young , bred by T F Nixon
See text describing the breeding .(**Note: incubation 24 to 26 days
for all Ring Necks)**

Some breeders claim to be able to look into a flight of grown chicks and to be absolutely certain in asserting that a particular chick came from a particular pair. This is very difficult to believe, especially when many birds are concerned.

There is only one way to be absolutely sure on this point, and that is to place split celluloid rings on the legs of the chicks before separating from the parents; thus leaving no doubt about the parents. The rings are put on by the use of a fluted metal tool which is supplied by the ringmakers.

PROBLEMS IN THE BREEDING SEASON

Desertion

One problem which may be encountered is that of the hen deserting the nest. There are a variety of reasons for desertion, and one very common cause is the lack of an adequate supply of green food. or fruit Another cause of desertion is lack of privacy for the sitting hens.

Nest boxes should not be placed too close to the windows of the bird room where the hens are presented with external distractions which may frighten them and cause them to leave the nest.

Unusual noises both inside and outside the bird room should be completely eliminated during breeding operations and it would be true to say that there are many experienced fanciers who will not allow visitors into their bird rooms while breeding is in progress.

Another theory on the problems of desertion is that the birds are not being offered sufficient vitamin supplements. Whether this is true or not is a matter of debate. Many fanciers believe that if the ordinary diet is well balanced the birds will obtain all the vitamins they require. Other breeders give vitamin supplements at breeding time in order to make sure that the birds have a good and regular supply.

As we have already noted, the weather may also play a part in causing the hens to desert their chicks.

Hand Rearing

Hand rearing is a very difficult and time consuming task, and although it would be true to say that chicks have been reared by hand, the chances of its succeeding are rather remote. If the hen has decided to desert the nest, then the first the fancier will know of it will be when he finds the chicks lying cold and obviously close to death in the bottom of the nest box.

If the chicks are found in this condition, then take them in cupped hands and breathe hard on them. This will bring them back to normal body temperature relatively quickly, at which point the process of handfeeding can begin.

Make up some bread and milk in a very sloppy mixture and take a small syringe of the type used by doctors, but without the needle. Take the chick in the left hand, and gently stroke the yellow part of the back of the beak with the end of the syringe, whereupon chick will gape for food. Insert only a little of the bread and milk mixture at a time, and when there is a reasonable amount of food in the crop, leave well alone. Give the chick plenty of time to pass the food into the crop before offering more. Forcing the food into the beak will result in blockage of the air passages and suffocation.

If, this situation arises, the chicks should be fed every hour except at night when they can be left from the fall of darkness, after the final feed, until dawn.

Some breeders use a sharpened matchstick to carry out the same operation, and either method will suffice. The important point is to get food into the crop of the chick as quickly as possible under the conditions described and no matter what method is used to achieve this end, it is justified if it is effective.

If the hen does desert the nest, and the chicks can be brought back to the point at which they are sufficiently strong to gape for food in the normal manner, then they should be transferred to another nest of chicks of similar age if this is possible. A hen which has deserted her nest rarely returns to it especially if the chicks have become weakened through lack of food. Under such circumstances there is a far greater possibility of their being reared by a foster hen than by the natural parents or by hand feeding.

One particular time at which hand feeding may be necessary is just before dusk, when the birds are beginning to settle down for the night. At that point, many breeders examine every nest and ensure that each chick has sufficient food in its crop, which can be very easily seen by looking at the translucent skin at the base of the neck. If the crop is empty then hand feeding must be attempted. If it is not, then the chances are that the chick will probably die of starvation during the night.

Breeding of the African Ring-Necked Parrakeet
Psittacula krameri krameri

Believed to be the first breeding of this species was recorded in 1960 (Avicultural Magazine, August 1960) by T.F. Nixon of Wisbech, Cambs.) A summary of his experiences is given below:

1. Purchased pair in 1975; were in a very poor condition with broken plumage.
2. After 2 years the birds began to look healthy with full plumage.
3. Spring of 1960 the birds started to take an interest in the nest box:
   Size 24" x l0" x l0" standing on a 4 foot post.*
4. Birds were very careful about being seen at the nest box. However, the hen was seen leaving the nest box early in April. The cock also went into the nest box at night.
5. Early May the box was inspected and three live chicks were found with one dead and one egg clear.
6. Feeding: Main diet sunflower and canary seed – they would not

*Some breeders use a larger box – it should be in a sheltered spot and made of thick wood to keep out the Winter cold.

accept fruit or greenstuff. With the chicks to feed the birds accep-
ted one sweet apple a day but the sunflower seed continued to
be the main diet.

7.   Weaning – chicks came out in June, one first week and the other
      at 4–5 day intervals. Almost fully grown, but without tail feathers
      which came in quite quickly when they started to fly.

      The beak was a very pale coral pink, which slowly turned first to
      bright red and then to blackish red.

8

WHEN AND WHAT TO FEED

HOW OFTEN?

Food and water are absolutely vital constituents in the life and well being of all birds. Get the diet right and much else will be satisfactory.

There are different points of view on how often birds should be fed and what they should be given. Moreover, each Genus and the related species does have a type of foot most suitable for its requirements, as near as possible to its natural food.

The form in which the food is fed should also be considered. For example Ring Necks with their powerful beaks will eat apples, oranges, grapefruits, carrots and other suitable fruit or vegetables without having to be cut. Simply spiking on a nail is adequate. When dealing with Grass Parrakeets (Turquoiseens), and Rosellas etc. fruit should be sliced or they are unlikely to touch it.

The pros and cons of daily feeding (once or twice per day) are as follows:

Advantages

1.   Birds learn to associate humans with food and look forward to receiving the due meal. This should lead to a closer relationship between captive and bird keeper. The birds can become quite tame.

It will be noted that hand reared parrots are much more expres -sive than aviary bred birds which are on the wild side. The tame birds learn to talk more easily.

2.   Fair shares should be possible for all and any that appear to be missing out can be given a supplementary feed.

SPECIAL NOTE In practice when the birds are kept quite hungry the weaker birds may starve so great care must be taken to see that none are

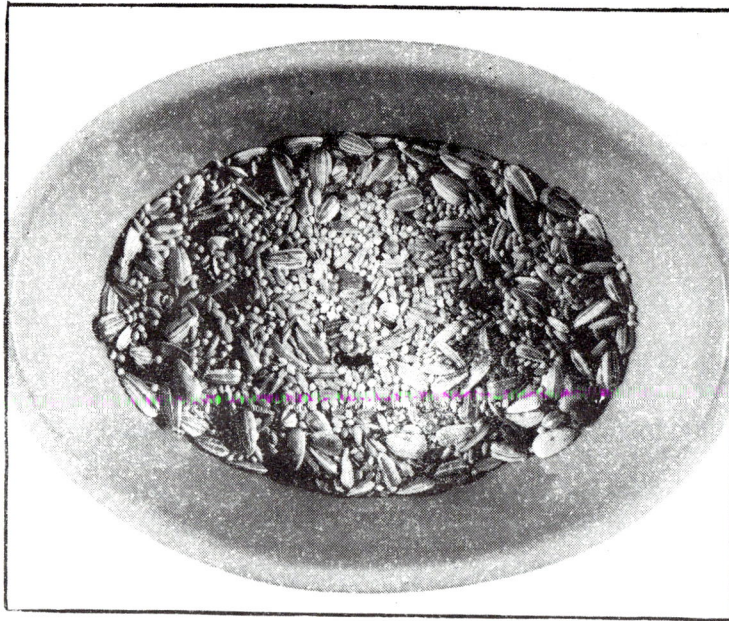

Mixed Seeds for Parrakeets

A, Plastic drinker;

B, Multipurpose food or water container;

Fig 7.3 Food and Related Equipment I

neglected.

3. Over feeding is avoided so the birds are fitter and more inclined to search for food in between meals.

4. Being hungry means that a varied and balanced diet will be taken quite readily.

5. Waste is minimised because the amount the birds eat quickly; say, 20 minutes.

The early morning meal would be given before 9.00 a.m. and the later one around 4.00 p.m., depending on weather and daylight available. The food is scattered where appropriate; e.g. on a bench or on the floor for ground feeding birds.

With Ring Necks a combination of the two methods would be appropriate. Remember also they like to eat sprouting seeds so a small amount of surplus should be allowed to scatter.

Possible disadvantages of daily feeding are as follows:

1. With a hobby fanciers do not always have the time to feed each day so a container of food is left which is sufficient for a few days.

2. Parrot-like birds prefer to eat early morning and late evening, but also take additional food during the day. Often they are reluctant to take food when being watched.

3. When some birds are bullied they will hang back and not be fed, but if a supply of seed is available will take it when others are not feeding.

In practice, with the hobbyist, a compromise is necessary. The basic seeds are left in a dish or dishes and extras are fed once a day. Thus apples and fruit are placed on spikes each day and titbits are given as required; e.g. millet sprays, soaked bread, greens.

WHAT TO FEED

Ring Necks will eat most normal parrot foods. Although pet shops sell Parrakeet mixture this is usually more suitable for the smaller species such as Grass Parrakeets. A more satisfactory method is to use a good quality Parrot mixture. This would include sunflower seed, peanuts, maize and various items such as peas and small peppers. If the birds will take canary seed – usually recommended but not always taken – this can be put in a separate dish. It is advisable to have separate dishes for doubtful items and then the consumption can be measured. Any new foods can be tested in this way.

Fasten with
Bull Dog Clip
to Upright in
Aviary

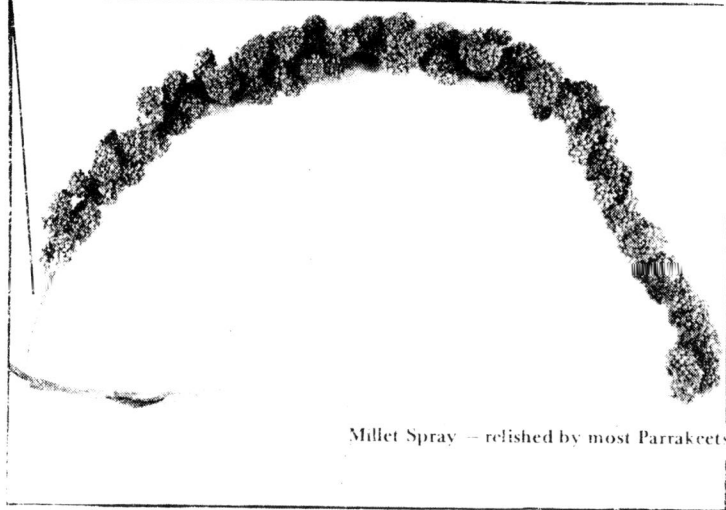

Millet Spray — relished by most Parrakeets

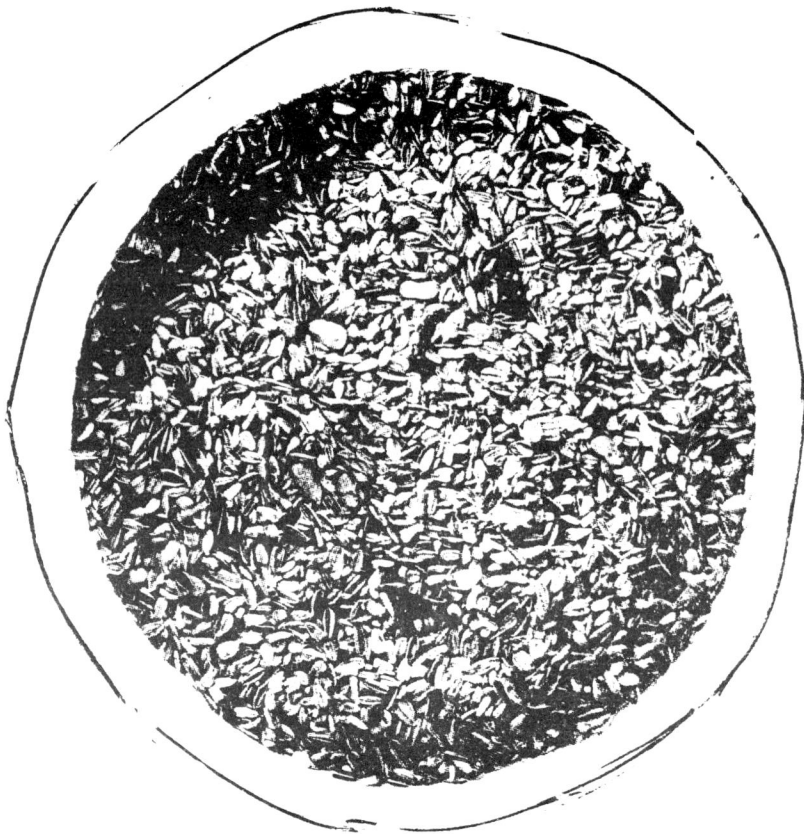

Fig . 7.3 Food and Related Equipment II

Possible Foods

1. Sunflower, maize, oats, wheat, peanuts, peas
2. Bread – soaked in milk or water or just plain
3. Apples, pears and other fruit
4. Green stuff such as chickweed and vegetable – carrots, turnips etc.

Some fanciers also try dog food (ground biscuit), poultry crumbs, and other pet foods.

In practice sunflower seed and fruit especially apples appear to be the main foodstuffs with the occasional millet spray and bunch of chickweed. However, variety is vital and the principles of feeding are explained in the next section.

Sprouting seeds are also given, especially when young are being reared. This may be done by using sprouting bowls or simply by throwing seeds on the earth floor and allowing them to germinate naturally; in a dry period spray them with water.

How Much Food

Attempts are sometimes made to specify how much food should be given to a species. This is very difficult because individual birds have preferences and may eat more of one type of food than another, leaving some seeds uneaten.

Many breeders have found that they eat a considerable amount of sunflower seed and fruit but little else. Yet desirably they should have roughage in the form of wholemeal bread. Accordingly, variety is essential, but minimising waste is also necessary. Piles of unwanted food leads to trouble and should be avoided.

If we assume as a rough guide that an adult Ring Neck will eat 50 grams each day (1–8oz) about 20 grams will be in sunflower seed. The balance will be sprouted seeds (including oats or wheat) – say 10 grams, peas and maize (say 5 grams) and the balance in wholemeal bread (5.8 grams) and the balance in titbits and various small seeds and other desirable foods.

The provision of grit and cuttlefish bone as well as water will be vital requirements in the feeding programme. Vitamin supplements should also be considered, but do not get carried away with this idea because a varied and ample diet should cover all essentials.

PRINCIPLES OF FEEDING

There now follows a factual coverage of the principles of sound feeding. It will help to show the bird-keeper why a varied diet is essential.

Even if sunflower seed is available in a trough try to give an added attraction each day – bread, apples, oranges, grapefruit, peanuts, green food and the occasional portion of poultry pellets or even dog food in flake form –

meat is not recommended.

FEEDING

VARIETY ESSENTIAL

As for all other parrot–like birds a variety of foods should be given. An understanding of food values is essential and as a background study some relevant notes are now given.

A fancier desires to have healthy birds and this means the correct environment and adequate food which usually means a balanced diet.

The essential components are as follows:

1. Proteins
2. Carbohydrates (starches)
3. Fats
4. Water

Food technology is now also able to specify the mineral content of foods but remembering a balanced diet is essential is good enough.

In order that a balanced diet can be calculated, it is necessary that the fancier should have some knowledge of the food content of the various seeds and other foods, following, which he will then be able to provide the essential balance. Below, is a table of seeds and other foods which sets out the constituents:

TABLE OF APPROXIMATE FOOD VALUES

	Water	Protein	Carbo-hydrate	Fat	%
Canary Seed	15.0	14.0	52.0	5.50	86.50
Rape Seed	7.0	22.0	20.0	40.0	89
Maw Seed	9.0	19.0	18.0	45.0	91
Millet Seed	14.0	15.0	57.0	4.0	93
Linseed	9.0	23.0	23.0	24.0	79
Hemp Seed	11.0	16.0	25.0	30.0	83
Niger Seed	12.0	21.0	22.0	40.0	95
Lettuce	95.0	1.0	2.0	0.2	99.2
Dandelion	84.0	2.4	10.6	1.0	
Carrot	87.0	1.2	9.6	0.1	
Apple	83.0	0.5	15.0	Nil	98.5
Egg Yolk	47.0	15.0	Nil	33.0	95
Egg White	87.0	10.0	Nil	0.25	97.25
Sunflower Seed	6.0	24.0	21.0	49.0	100

BASIC CONSTITUENTS

There are three basic constituents necessary in the diet of all living creatures; namely, proteins, carbohydrates and fats. These three elements must be contained in any given diet, and what is more important, they must be balanced against each other if all of the dietary requirements of the birds are to be met.

Protein

It is frequentiy, and perhaps correctly, argued that protein is the most essential constituent in the diet of any type of bird life. Protein is the substance which builds the muscles and which will quite literally put the meat on the bones.

Carbohydrates

Another essential part of the diet is the carbohydrate content. This is the dietary element which gives energy and which is used up rapidly by the body processes, especially when excrcise is being taken, rather in the same way as coal is consumed in a fire.

Fats within Food

Fats are another important part of the diel. These elements supploment the carbohydrates and also generate body heat. However, excessive amounts can be harmful.

From this information, it can clearly be seen that the emphasis on a balanced diet cannot be stressed too strongly. What, for example, is the point in giving a diet which is overloaded witll protein, if the carbohydrates are insufficient to burn up the excess proteins? In such a case, the result would be obesity in the stock rather than a balanced type of bird. Pieces of fat are not recommended.

SPECIAL NOTES

1. **Growing feathers, beaks, toenails require an extra amount of protein and, therefore, young birds should be given a special diet containing a high level of protein,**

2. **Amino Acids** are essential for growth and, therefore, must be present in the diet. A variety of seeds is essential for the bird to achieve the level of amino acids it requires.

3. **Vitamins** These are essential to the well being of seed eaters. They are:
   a)   Vitamin A – fish liver oil is the best source; but greens and carrots are also essential and are taken readily. A deficiency will result in

poor breeding results, constant colds (breathing difficulties), water eyes and thick mucous around the nostrils.

Cod–liver oil should be mixed daily with the seed and the wild green listed later. In addition, lettuce, spinach, kale and other fresh greens should be given. Bleached vegetables should not be given and cabbage or brussels sprouts do not give a high level of vitamin A.

b) Vitamin D – Lack of vitamin D results in leg, joint, beak and other bone growth problems (rickets) Adding cod liver oil and feeding calcium in some form will help to combat the deficiency, but sun shine is the essential requirement. The ultra violet rays from the sun are vital and special lamps can provide rays, but may damage the eyes of the birds due to being too strong. Sunshine through clean glass is not helpful because the ultra violet rays may not pass through.

c) Vitamin E – This vitamin provides the necessary component for reproduction. Its main source is sprouting seeds such as wheat and certain leaf plants such as lettuce, watercress and spinach. Egg yolk is also a prime source. However, wheatgerm oil should be mixed separately from cod–liver oil, although the two can be used on seed provided they are mixed separately.

d) Water–soluble Vitamins – Many vitamins may be purchased in the form of a soluble solution such as *Abidec* and many fanciers find that this method is adequate. However, greenstuff and egg food are still vital and should not be omitted.

IMPORTANCE OF FRESH SEED

If poor quality seed is used the birds will starve or will suffer from diseases of one sort or another. A seed is made up of a number of parts:

a) Shell
b) Embryo (proteins and vitamins, etc.)
c) Endosperm (starchesl

SPECIAL NOTE

Each seed is a living organism which should be capable of germinating; if not then it should not be fed to birds. The first part to deteriorate is usually the germ part (the embryo) which contains the proteins and ,without which ,a bird will suffer various ill effects , such as running eyes – eventually it will starve.

Problems with seeds which are deteriorating are as follows:

a)   Infested with mould and fungi.
b)   Contaminated with chemicals or oil due to faulty storage.
c)   Mixed with dust and/or other undesirable elements, including mite
     or weevils.
d)   Smelling musty or rancid.
e)   Too old or kept in warm humid conditions. A cool well ventilated
     atmosphere is desirable.

SPROUTING SEEDS

Many bird fanciers believe wholeheartedly that sprouted seed should be integral part of the diet of cage birds. It is agreed that sprouting reduces the starch and increases the protein and , in addition ,makes the seed more easily digested. They spend hours each month preparing and feeding the sprouted seeds and certainly many birds seem to relish the wet food.

In recent times doubt has been cast on the wisdom of using sprouted seed and whilst there is not conclusive proof that the practice is harmful the following facts should be considered:

1.   Soaking brings about a chemical reaction in the seed and changes
     the starch to sugar. This in itself is not harmful but if the seeds are left
     in the water, without adequate exposure to the air, they begin to
     deteroriate. In fact, if left longer than 24 hours the seed will begin
     to die. An experiment out in the USA found that birds fed with
     seeds soaked for 48 hours would not lay.

2.   Many of the proteins may be released into the water.

3.   From observations made it would appear that soaked seeds do
     not digest properly. Soaking appears to give them some kind
     of protection against the digestive juices; in fact, nestlings fed
     by their parents will usually pass the soaked seeds through   their
     system without any change in composition.

SPECIAL NOTE:
Most of the arguments are against badly soaked seeds so any to be soaked should be germinated on a stainless steel or plastic dish and kept *damp* not soaked) by means of gauze which rests in water. Absolute cleanliness is

BREEDING ROOM REGISTER

PEN No. . . . . COCK . . . . HEN . . . .

First Egg Laid	Hen Set	Due to Hatch	No. of Young	Remarks

PEN No. . . . . COCK . . . . HEN . . . .

First Egg Laid	Hen Set	Due to Hatch	No. of Young	Remarks

Register which shows all essentials for each hen

Fig. 7.4 Breeding Records

essential to avoid contamination.

CONDITIONS REQUIRING DIFFERENT OR SUPPLEMENTED FOOD

When feeding birds it is essential to consider the following:

1. Normal feeding for healthy stock.
2. Feeding for breeding.
3. Food for moulting.
4. Supplements or special food for periods of stress, e.g. when moulting or when sick.

NORMAL FEEDING

The comments made earlier apply to this situation. A *balanced* diet is essential and feed regularly so that the birds have ample food without standing around too long.

When dealing with domesticated birds such as poultry we can state precisely what quantity is necessay for growing, laying and so on. Around 4oz. per laying hen will be fed. This is a precise measure. However, with cage birds the amount eaten is not proportionate to the relative weight of fowl and, say, canaries or, parrots . Some food they will peck out of the hopper, others they will leave and there is no standardisation as for poultry.

A parrot prefers different food from a budgerigar although they belong to the same family. Each bird fancier must find out the likes and dislikes of his birds and feed accordingly.

FOOD FOR MOULTING

A great deal is written about the problems of the moult and yet in the correct environment there is generally no problem. The fact remains that the growing of feathers requires extra protein and vitamins. Soft food is usually recommended and tonic seeds should also be given.

The annual shedding of feathers takes place as the weather changes and becomes colder. In the UK this occurs around the middle of September and goes on for a few weeks; it may occur earlier or later, but usually an attempt is made to have birds back in condition for the November shows.

Some fanciers have special cages for moulting birds, whereas others simply separate the cocks. When birds are transferred they should be taken in pairs or threes so they are placed in their new abode together thus avoiding conflict when single birds are placed in a cage at different times.

At the *early stages* of the moulting period feed a plain diet and water until feathers begin to fall. A bird is through the moult when the new head feathers are fully grown.

Soft food should be given twice weekly. During the moult there should be adequate ventilation and moderate exercise. A plentiful supply of the greenstuff is essential.

Additional Notes

For the novice additional notes are now added compiled by a well known bird keeper:

1. Green Food
    Some breeders advocate a liberal supply of green food for breeding birds, while others look upon it as little short of a deadly poison; and here it may be remarked that both sides are right to a certain extent, for much depends upon the kind and quality of the green stuff supplied to the birds.
    Nature provides a valuable part of the supplementary food required by Parrakeets. Greenstuff is a vital part of the diet and wild seeds help to provide oil and other essentials tor beautiful plumage.
    The main green foods are as follows:

    (a) Chickweed which is very popular and nutritious (although some fanciers do not like to feed chick weed)
    (b) Dandelion which provides many essentials such as calcium, iron and magnesium
    (c) Mustard seed
    (d) Plantain
    (e) Shepherd's purse
    (f) Teazle
    (g) Dock

    A little should be given once a day and should be varied to stimulate the appetite.
    Important: wild seeds are those taken from dock, maw, presacaria, gold of pleasure and plantain.

2. Basic Foods
    Food stuffs of seeds of various types supplemented with vitamins, oils and minerals. In addition, wild plants and fruit should be given on a regular basis, thus keeping the birds in peak condition.
    A balanced diet is essential and this should be formulated on the basis of whether dealing with birds for breeding or when moulting, or for normal feeding.

Birds will acquit themselves of their parental duties to the satisfaction of their owner. But sometimes they will not, and it is only fair to say that there are birds that no plan or system of feeding will induce to attend to their offspring for more than a few days, or a week or two at the outside.

SOAKED SEED.

So far so good; now we come to the most important part of the system. The seed – the best quality obtainable – is to be put to soak in cold fresh water. When taken from the vessel in which it has been soaked, the seed should be wiped dry in a towel or other cloth or it should be strained thoroughly as part of the process. If this precaution is neglected the seed will stick together in a lump, will be difficult for the birds to get at, and will, moreover, be liable to turn sour. The seed must be prepared from day to day and if put to soak in the morning, when the birds are being attended to, will be ready by the same hour on the following day, Regularity in this respect reduces the "trouble" to a minimum.

SEED–HOPPERS

Several kinds of seed–hoppers have been invented, with the object of guarding against waste. Many birds make a practice of scattering their seed – in search, no doubt, of something of which they are in want – and these hoppers are useful in their way, but as much care is necessary to keep the contents clean and free from dust in their case as in that of the ordinary kind. The type of dish preferred by the author is a large open and shallow type which allows maximum exposure of seeds (Ring Necks are not scratchers like Kakarikis so burying of seed is not advisable). See Fig 7.3 for drawing of 2 ft. wide dish – a similar container serves as as a water container for drinking or bathing . This is filled by using a hose and is cleaned weekly with a soft scrubbing brush.

WATER

An important point, and one that is too often overlooked, is to keep the drinking water pure and clean, for birds, especially when bread or eggs are fed, are apt to quickly spoil it by dipping their beaks into the fountain or cup while particles of food are still adhering to their mandibles. It will be as well, particularly in hot weather, to change the water and cleanse the vessel that holds it several times a day, for the particles of egg and other food quickly decompose, and are apt to give rise to trouble some diarrhoea in both old and young.

GRIT

Calcium is essential for the development of egg shells and as part of diet. In addition, insoluble grit must be provided for digesting the food; e.g

·flint at the appropriate size.

The mixture to be given should include:

1.   Cuttle–fish bone
2.   Washed river sand
3.   Oyster shell
4.   Charcoal finely ground

GETTING THE CORRECT BALANCE

As noted above , the typical foods contain different proportions of protein, carbohydrates and fat. Getting the correct balance is important but also difficult.

Like humans, birds have periods when they like one form of food rather than another. The weather, time of year, whether breeding or moulting all make a difference.The author finds that citrus fruits, such as grapefruits are eaten only in the summer months.

In addition ,there is habit – what foods have been fed in the past, espec-ially in the early stages of development. When new birds are acquired there is always difficulty in getting the mixture correct and, indeed, it is advis-able to ask the previous owner for details of the diet.

The vital foods also include various fruits, greens and softfood as described earlier.

BASIC RULES – SUMMARY

1.   **Feed on a regular basis and clear husks away every few
       days.**
       Some bird keepers maintain a small collection of other birds such as doves, quail ,or bantams which clear away discarded food. Obviously a large enough aviary will be essential.

2.   **Provide an adequate and varied diet:
       (a) Mixed seeds and nuts**

       (b) Fruit; e.g. Pears, grapes and apples, bananas, blackberries
            and dates

       (c) Softfood such as stale bread – not mouldy, **soaked** and then
            the liquid pressed out to make it crumbly (not doughy) or egg
            food (hard boiled egg sliced and mixed with bread crumbs)

       (d) Green foods such as:
            (i) lettuce, spinach and garden peas
            (ii) wild plants and seeds there from, including chick–weed, dock,
            persicaria and plantain

e) Root vegetables; eg, carrots

(f) Soaked seeds and also sprouting seeds

. Do not leave food around too long and feed fresh fruit which is not too ripe. Bananas which have gone to pulp are frequently seen in aviaries and are unattractive to most birds.

3. Provide other essentials such as:
(a) Grit, cuttlefish bone, etc.
(b) Water
(c) Vitamins

4. Use suitable food and water utensils so food is not wasted.

SEED MIXTURES

As a rough guide it is usual to divide mixtures as follows:

1 Parrots and Parrakeets
(Macaws, Amazons, Cockatoos, African Greys, Ring Necks etc)

Give a mixture consisting of large nutritious foods such as sunflower seeds, nuts, maize, hemp, canary seed, millet, wheat and niger.

Opinions differ on the proportions. Sunflower seeds should form a substantial part. One well known breeder suggests 65% ,whereas another believes that 40% is about right with the balance being made up of canary seed and other food.

For example:

Grey Parrot

Canary   30
Millet   5
Hemp   5
Sunflower 50
Oats   5
Peanuts__ 5_
                    100%

This mixture is supplied or can be mixed for the larger Parrots ,but ,whilst adequate, Ring Necks prefer a diet of Sunflower seeds ,Peanuts and Apples above all else. It is essential to also provide extras on a daily basis to augment this basic diet which is available at all times.

2. Parrakeets and Smaller Parrots
(eg, Parrakeets, Lovebirds, Kakarikis, Cockatiels)

A similar mixture to the above , but with more of the smaller seeds. The smaller birds should not be given too much sunflower seed or hemp.

Example:

	%
Canary	50
Millet	20
Peanuts	10
Sunflower	10
Safflower	10
	100%

Some seed shops sell this sort of mixture for all Parrakeets, but Ring Necks usually prefer a Parrot–type mixture.

5. Provide a bath so that birds can splash around and bathe themselves.

All food should be clean and wholesome. Fruit such as apples should be placed on spikes; eg, nails, so they cannot roll around the aviary.

Greenstuffs should be rinsed to remove possible m eggs of worms or other parasites and also to eliminate any chemicals where the plants may have been sprayed. Badly frosted greens should not be fed.

BEHAVIOUR OF RING NECKS WHEN FEEDING

Ring Necks in a communal aviary are rather like children, boisterous and constantly trying to get the best advantage. They will fly on to a perch and eat a spiked and another wil l come along and push the first bird off the perch. Usually this is all good natured squabbling. Occasionally they try to grab each other, but one will avoid the attack and the incident passes off very quickly .

Soaked seeds are thrown on the floor and induced to sprout by allowing rain to enter the aviary (an open top) or by spraying water on to them when the water containers are filled. The birds then eat the sprouting shoots.

orange colour, but the mutations vary; the Lutino has a pinky glow and others have a very light eye. I have one hen with a white iris. It has been that cock birds have a slightly grey tinge in the yellow, but this is very difficult to detect without close examination.

LUTINO

The Lutino applies to the Indian Ring Necks including the Alexandrine. It does not appear to have been produced in the African species which is less popular than the Indian forms.

Dr. W.T. Greene writing in 1898 stated:

" There is a very pretty variety of this bird, of a rich canary colour throughout, but as it is rare it is, of course, very valuable. It is a true albino not withstanding its bright yellow colour, for it has pink eyes........".

Since that time more information has been gathered and a better understanding is possible. A white bird is very difficult to breed; indeed impossible from the standard green colour. Instead a "coloured white" appears, influenced by the Green and becoming yellow. Pure Albinos have been produced but these involve a difficult colour combination, discussed later.

SEX LINKED

If a male Lutino is mated to a Normal female the offspring should be **females** Lutino and **males** Green. On average there should be 50 per cent males and 50 per cent females, but this is unlikely to occur in individual hatches so a number of nests will have to be taken together for the statistical average to work out.

A male, having two sex chromosomes, may have Lutino linked to one or both ;ie, be split when linked to one, and a visible mutation if linked to both.

The female does not have two sex chromosomes and, therefore, is either Green or Lutino, whichever factor is linked to the single chromosome. It follows that the hen will not be a split Lutino.

POSSIBLE MATCHINGS

1. Lutino cock x Lutino hen = LC + LH (50:50)
2. Lutino cock x Normal hen = LCN (Split) + LH (50:50)
3. Split cock x Lutino hen = LC + LH + SC + NH (25% of each)
4. Split cock x Normal hen = LH + NH + SC + NC (25% each)
5. Normal cock x Lutino hen = SC (Normal) + NH (No Lutinos)

In planning a breeding programme for maximising on Lutinos it be necessary to take the pairings which are likely to give the most yellows.

Thus:

Lutino cock x Lutino female = all Lutinos

Lutino cock x Normal female = 50% Lutino females

Split cock x Lutino Female = 25% of Lutino males and 25% Lutino females

* For an interesting article on Ring Neck Parrakeets and their mutations : Jim Hayward , *Cage and Aviary Birds*, 3rd June 1989

This summary of possible mating expectations is much simplified. Unfortunately we are not aware of the background of many of the birds used for breeding. Our "mutations" may be a single breeding, a "freak", never to be reproduced again. The so-called Splits may have little chance of producing the colour believed to be carried. Anyone with experience of colour breeding will know that unrelated strains may produce all kinds of results from colours hidden away for generations. This atavism or reversion brings about many surprises. Despite what is sometimes suggested the breeding of different colour mutations is not an exact science and with Ring Necks the problems are immense.

BLUES

Blue Ring Necks are notoriously difficult to breed other than from Blues, but they continue to increase in numbers. They are no longer in the rare mutation category. If sufficient cash is available there should be no problem in obtaining a pair of Blue Ring Necks. Blues are an overall blue colour of a beautiful even shade. The neck markings for mature cock birds are the same as for Normal Greens. Various percentages can be estimated as before although, unlike the Lutino, the Blues are not sex linked.

Thus;

1. Blue cock x Blue hen = 100% Blue
2. Green x Blue = 50% Green/Blue, 25% Green, 25% Blue
3. Green/Blue x Green = 50% Green; 50% Green/Blue
4. Green/Blue x Green/Blue = 25% Green; 25% Blue; 50% Green/ Blue

GREYS

Greys of the correct shade are a good even colour. Exactly how Greys have been produced is shrouded in mystery, but possibly came from a single bird with the Grey factor. However, birds of a clear Grey colour are likely to have been crossed with Blue Ring Necks at some state; i.e. Blue will be in the make-up.

In terms of inheritance the Grey is a dominant colour mutation. This means that once the colour is available the breeding of further Greys is feasible because mating to a Normal Green will produce some Greys.

The chromosomes may be in 'single' or 'double' for the Grey colour. This fact will affect the outcome of the breeding results. When the double factor is present the chance of success in producing Greys is very high.

Thus:

1. Grey x Grey (double factor) = 100% Grey
2. Grey x Grey (single factor) = 50% Grey (single factor) 25% Grey (double factor), 25% Green
3. Grey (double factor) x Green = 100% Grey
4. Grey (single factor) x Grey (double factor) = 50% (double factor):50% (single)
5. Grey (single factor) x Green = 50% Grey (single factor); 50% Green

EXERCISE AND HEALTH

Flying from one part of the aviary to another should be encouraged; exercise is vital for fitness and breeding. Giving adequate perches of a wide variety should be the aim. Remember Ring Necks spend their natural lives in trees and gnaw the branches. Try to simulate these conditions so they live happily.

Put the food in different places so that they have to fly around to reach the different titbits whether apple, chickweed, celery, carrots, or seeds. They are not battery hens so variety is essential. Often you will *not* see them feeding so watch to see what is taken.

9

BREEDING DIFFERENT COLOURS

It is essential to recognise that there are true mutations and also colours which **appear by chance**, which the breeder must then seek to stabilise by breeding back to one of the parents, in the hope that further specimens are bred. Once a number of a specific colour have been bred the mutation is on the way to becoming established. It must be possible to breed true on a consistent basis to be able to claim that a proper mutation is present.

A knowledge of **genetics** and **colour types** will assist in arriving at new mutations, but regretfully much is pure chance. The dedicated fancier who sees a strange colour in the fledglings should nurture the bird in question and hope it will reach maturity so that it can be bred from. With Ring Necks this can be a slow process so creating a new mutation can take many years; hence the very high prices paid for new colours when they become available.

COLOUR MUTATIONS

Colour mutations are now well established in many aviary birds. Often they are the result of an accidental breeding of an "off colour" which is then retained and inbred in the hope of establishing the particular colour as a specific mutation. For recognition as a mutation the colour must be capable of breeding true and consistently. Unfortunately, this condition is not always met even with established mutations. With Ring Necks many of the mutations are not yet fully established. Even some of the common forms – Lutinos and Blues – will not always come true. The fancier who purchases "splits" in the hope of breeding the mutation colour is often disappointed and finds that the standard green colour is produced rather than yellow or blue.

SPLITS

The term "split" is used to denote a condition where a pair of genes do not match up, although a non-standard colour is present. Thus in Ring

Plate 3: Ring Neck Parrakeets; Fallow Cock
Grey Hen (Top)

Prue Francis

Plate 4: Ring Neck Parrakeets; Cinnamon Cock (Top)
Olive Hen (Bottom)

Necks the normal colour is green ,but if the paired structure (the chromosomes) do not match, althoughgreen will still be the colour there isthe hidden colour, say, yellow which may appear in its pure form when both genes carry the yellow.

Both genes being identical is referred to as **homozygous**; i.e. same colour.

Where they differ they are **heterozygous** and would be described as; for example:

Split--Green/Blue.

This means the bird is carrying a Blue gene and may produce some Blues. In practice, a very long wait may be experienced before the elusive new colour appears; sometimes it never occurs.

DETERMINATION OF SEX

The Phenotype of the offspring is determined by the genes which the young bird has inherited from its parents, and similar remarks apply to the determination of its sex. In genetics, the chromosomes are described diagramatically as X and Y. The chromosomes of the male so far as sex determination is concerned are both of the X type. The female carries one X and one Y chromosome, the Y chromosome being the determining factor in the reproduction of female young.

When the new sex cells are being formed, the chromosomes split and travel to opposite sides of the new cells. In the male, both new cells will carry an X chromosome, but in the female, one new cell will carry an X chromosome and the other will carry the female Y chromosome. If a male cell then comes into contact with an X carrying cell from the hen, the resulting chick will be a male. If the chromosome which carries the X factor from the male comes into contact with a cell carrying a Y factor chromosome from the hen, then the resulting chick will be female.

COCK 'S CHROMOSOME   **HEN'S CHROMOSOME**

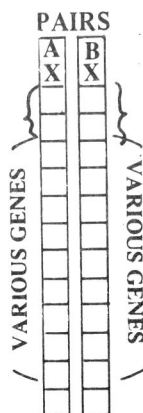

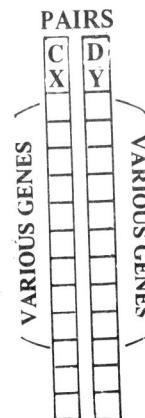

Chromosomes in Birds – the female determines the sex

COLOURS BRED
Colours which may be found and purchased are:
1. **Normal Green**
2. **Yellow (Lutinos)**
3. **Blues**
4. **Albinos**

In addition, various "off colours" have been produced in the U.S. A., on the Continent and in Britain. They may be as follows:
1. Grey (now well established) .
2. Olive
3. Cinnamon.
4. Turquoise Blue.
5. Deep Yellow.
6. Pied.
7. Deep Blue / Mauve.
8. White – Yellow or Blue Bred.

Opinions differ on what each colour really represents. When does a "fallow" become an "olive". What is a "Lutino" and when does this become a "deep yellow" or "primrose".

In the "off colours" a wide variety of permutations may be possible. There may be a yellow head on a green or blue body. Another possibility would be an inter–mingling of colours. This is different from a Pied which usually takes the form of a mixture of colours in distinct sections.   The novice is quite bewildered by some of the colour descriptions which may be found in aviculture. Whether a colour is dominant, recessive or sex–linked (one sex only producing a specific colour) may be of vital importance in the descriptions. Ring Necks which are dominant for normal green may be split for another colour, say, Lutino and, therefore, may be able to produce Lutino progeny. Thus such a bird would be described as Normal **Green** / **Lutino**; i.e. Normal split for Lutino. The likelihood of producing a specific mutation is discussed below.

NORMAL COLOURS (GREEN)

The normal colour of Ring Necks, including Alexandrines, is green in a variety of shades. In practice , they vary quite considerably and when selecting a bird aim for those with bright colours, with strong wings and a long tail of the full length; far too many birds finish up with stunted tails due to the birds being allowed to live in unsuitable conditions; e.g. tail touching ground which is soiled.

Ring Necks have beautiful tail feathers with all colours blending together so any that look bedraggled are not in accordance with the normal standard.

Eye colour varies a little; the irides tends to be a pale yellow or pale orange colour, but the mutations vary; the Lutino has a pinky glow and others have a very light eye. I have one hen with a white iris. It has been that cock birds have a slightly grey tinge in the yellow, but this is very difficult to detect without close examination.

LUTINO

The Lutino applies to the Indian Ring Necks including the Alexandrine. It does not appear to have been produced in the African species which is less popular than the Indian forms.

Dr. W.T. Greene writing in 1898 stated:

" There is a very pretty variety of this bird, of a rich canary colour throughout, but as it is rare it is, of

course, very valuable. It is a true albino not withstanding its bright yellow colour, for it has pink eyes.......".

Since that time more information has been gathered and a better understanding is possible. A white bird is very difficult to breed; indeed impossible from the standard green colour. Instead a "coloured white" appears, influenced by the Green and becoming yellow. Pure Albinos have been produced but these involve a difficult colour combination, discussed later.

SEX LINKED

It a male Lutino is mated to a Normal female the offspring should be **females** Lutino and **males** Green. On average there should be 50 per cent males and 50 per cent females, but this is unlikely to occur in individual hatches so a number of nests will have to be taken together for the stat-istical average to work out.

A male, having two sex chromosomes, may have Lutino linked to one or both ; ie, be split when linked to one, and a visible mutation if linked to both.

The female does not have two sex chromosomes and, therefore, is either Green or Lutino, whichever factor is linked to the single chromosome. It follows that the hen will not be a split Lutino.

POSSIBLE MATCHINGS
1. Lutino cock x Lutino hen = LC + LH (50:50)
2. Lutino cock x Normal hen = LCN (Split) + LH (50:50)
3. Split cock x Lutino hen = LC + LH + SC + NH (25% of each)
4. Split cock x Normal hen = LH + NH + SC + NC (25% each)
5. Normal cock x Lutino hen = SC (Normal) + NH (No Lutinos)

In planning a breeding programme for maximising on Lutinos it be necessary to take the pairings which are likely to give the most yellows. **Thus:**

Lutino cock x Lutino female = all Lutinos
Lutino cock x Normal female = 50% Lutino females
Split cock x Lutino Female = 25% of Lutino males and 25% Lutino females

* For an interesting article on Ring Neck Parrakeets and their mutations : Jim Hayward , *Cage and Aviary Birds*, 3rd June 1989

This summary of possible mating expections is much simplified. Unfortunatelywe are not aware of the background of many of the birds used for breeding. Our "mutations" may be a single breeding, a "freak", never to be reproduced again. The so-called Splits may have littlechance of producing the colour believed to be carried. Anyone with experience of colour breeding will know that unrelated strains may produce all kinds of results from colours hidden away for generations. This atavism or reversion brings about many surprises. Despite what is sometimes suggested the breeding of different colour mutations is not an exact science and with Ring Necks the problems are immense.

BLUES

Blue Ring Necks are notoriously difficult to breed otherthan from Blues, but they continue to increase in numbers. They are no longer in the rare mutation category. If sufficient cash is available there should be no problem in obtaining a pair of Blue Ring Necks. Blues are an overall blue colour of a beautiful even shade. The neck markings for mature cock birds are the same as for Normal Greens. Various percentages can be estimated as before although, unlike the Lutino, the Blues are not sex linked.

Thus;

1. Blue cock x Blue hen = l00% Blue
2. Green xBlue =50% Green/Blue ,25% Green, 25% Blue
3. Green/Blue x Green = 50% Green; 50% Green/Blue
4. Green/Blue x Green/Blue = 25% Green; 25% Blue; 50% Green/ Blue

GREYS

Greys of the correct shade are a good even colour. Exactly how Greys have been produced is shrouded in mystery, but possibly came from a single bird with the Grey factor. However, birds of a clear Grey colour are likely to have been crossed with Blue Ring Necks at some state; i.e. Blue will be in the make-up.

In terms of inheritance the Grey is a dominant colour mutation. This means that once the colour is available the breeding of further Greys is feasible because mating to a Normal Green will produce some Greys.

The chromosomes may be in 'single' or ' double' for the Grey colour. This fact will affect the outcome of the breeding results. When the double factor is present the chance of success in producing Greys is very high.

Thus:

1. Grey x Grey (double factor) = 100% Grey
2. Greyx Grey (single factor) = 50% Grey (single factor) 25%Grey (double factor), 25% Green
3. Grey (double factor) x Green= l00% Grey
4. Grey (singlefactor) x Grey (doublefactor)=50% (doublefactor):50% (single)
5. Grey (single factor) x Green = 50% Grey (single factor); 50% Green

ALBINOS

Albinos are pure white, lacking any pigment. As noted earlier from the Normal Green they appear as Lutinos. Obviously they must be produced from other mutations such as Blue. Examples of possible matings are:

1. Blue cock x Lutino hen = Albino hens + Blue cocks/Lutino
2. Lutino/Blue cock x Blue hen = Albino hens, Lutino/Blue hens, Blue/Albino cocks, Green/Blue/Albino cocks
3. Blue/Albino cock x Blue hen = Albino hens, Blue hens, Blue/Albino cock and Blue cocks

Some breeders recommend using 2 above because this gives a 25 per cent chance of obtaining an Albino, either male or female.

DATES OF CAPTIVE BREEDING

The actual or approximate date of the first successful breeding is given below. It will be appreciated that not all breeding results are made public so there is no guarantee of the accuracy; furthermore, great success has been achieved in Belgium, Holland and Germany where details are not always known.

African Ring Neck (Normal)	1960
Indian Ring Neck (Normal)	1850
Lutino	1880 (approx.)
Blue	1920s
Albino	1963
Grey	Late 1970s
Fallow	1980
Alexandrine	1884

NOTE ON COLOURS

Further notes on the new colour mutations may assist the bird fancier. However, it should be stressed that these should not be taken as statement of absolute or likely occurrences. Our knowledge of breeding Ring Necks is not adequate enough to predict with certainty the outcome of specific crosses.

1. Consistent breeding of specific colour.

Breeding one colour with another will usually produce the same colour.

However, if the colours are Split then some other colour may emerge.

2. Primary Breeding

Certain colours can be bred together and the outcome fairly certain. Others will result from crossing one mutation with another or even Split mutations, one with the other. Thus the following appeared in a recent magazine "For Sale" column:

> **SALE Ringnecks: outstanding pr., Cock**
> **Blue/Lutino, hen Lutino/Blue (will produce Albino).**
> **£ ... a pr.**

3. Colour Recognition

At present some of the colours in Ring Necks are unstable and difficult to define with certainty. Yet the same colours are stabilised with other parrot-like species. Examples:

(a) Olive

Olives should be a dark olive green colour. As shown by the painting on the colour plates this olive colour is still not evenly distributed. In lovebirds a dark olive green is called "jade" and no doubt this will be bred in Ring Necks in due course.

Olives are sometimes referred to as **double-factor** birds a reference to the gene requirement for breeding them.

(b) Cinnamon

A Cinnamon varies in colour tremendously ranging from a browny green to a rich buttercup yellow often with a darker colour on the wings (a cinnamon brown on flights). Ideally it should be a cinnamon colour throughout.

(c) Fallow

This appears to be a mixture of colours, but strictly it should be a fawn colour or reddish yellow. It will be seen that a liberal interpretation is placed on the colour by Parrakeet breeders. The dark green wings possibly misrepresent the ideal. (see colour plate)

THE PARROT SOCIETY

Those interested in parrot-like birds are advised to join The Parrot Society, IO8b Fenlake Road, Bedford, MK4 OEU, England

BIBLIOGRAPHY

Birds of Burma B.A . Smythies, Nimrod Press,1986

Parrots and Parrot-like Birds , Marquess of Tavistock

Encyclopaedia of Aviculture A.Rutgers and K.A. Norris
Blandford ,1977
A large 3 volume set with volume 2 covering Parrots and Parrakeets.

Parrots,   W. de Grahl, Ward Lock, 1981
A concise and very readable book on the Parrot Family.

Parrots,   C.H. Rogers, Muller, 1953
A basic text for absolute beginners.

Foreign Bird Keeping,   Illiffe , 1902

Foreign Birds for Cage and Aviary Arthur G. Butler (n.d.)
Two volumes   Part II dealing with parrots (out of print)

Parrots of the World ,   J.M. Forshaw, Landsdowne,
Melbourne 1973
Very fine paintings by Wm. T. Cooper

The Foreigner,   various dates
A magazine devoted to foreign bird keeping in the pre-1939 period.

Also bound copies of Aviculture issued by The Aviculture Society.

Cage and Aviary Birds, Reed Business Publishing
The main British magazine on aviculture and essential reading for all interested in cage birds.

INDEX